DELPHIE'S TRUNK

Patricia McCall Corlew

Library of Congress Control Number: 2010911582
ISBN: Hardcover   978-1-4535-5250-6
                 Softcover   978-1-4535-5249-0
                 Ebook   978-1-4535-5251-3

This book was printed in the United States of America.

To order additional copies of this book, contact:
Xlibris Corporation
1-888-795-4274
www.Xlibris.com
Orders@Xlibris.com
81002

CONTENTS

Dedicated to **Delphia Omega Owen McCall**,
my paternal Grandmother, *keeper of the trunk,*
and to **Charles Allen McCall, Sr.,**
my Father, *author of the letters.*

for my nieces and nephews
**Casi, Erin, Logan, Matthew,
McKenzie, Megan, Michelle and Ricky**

July 20, 2009

My Dear Ones,

Today marks the 90th birthday of my Father, your Grandpa Charlie. You never knew him, for he died too soon, before any of you were born. Had he lived and been whole, I know he would have delighted in each and every one of you. To honor his memory, I am embarking on a literary journey into the essence of your Grandfather. Through the letters found in our Grandma Delphie's trunk, I am hoping to weave a story of my Father, of who and what he was. I invite you into the past times and places of Grandpa Charlie's world. May your own life's journey be enriched by knowing his.

Love always,
Aunt Pat

ACKNOWLEDGEMENTS

In addition to the military records, magazines, newspaper clippings, and abundant memorabilia from her Grandmother's trunk, the author also obtained information from the following websites: *Navsource.org/archives; Military History Online; Time Magazine Archives* and *Wikipedia.* Authors quoted are cited with their respective quotes.

PROLOGUE

Our Grandmother McCall was a very spiritual woman. She was also very religious. While these can be, they are not necessarily the same. This past autumn I had an encounter which speaks to both of these attributes.

Each fall for many years, around the end of October and All Saints Day, I have visited the graves of our McCall family ancestors in the cemetery of the tiny, rural Oak Grove Baptist Church in the beautiful Western North Carolina Mountains. Several families are buried in this sacred place. Tombstones mark the graves of six generations of McCalls. Your Grandpa Charlie's and Grandma Alice's remains are there beneath a double headstone. These annual pilgrimages, each unique, have been profound experiences evoking in me a sense of awe, thanksgiving and respect. This past autumn of 2008, was especially poignant. The cemetery is tended by the church which keeps the grass mown and the leaves raked. However, the footstones are always overgrown with grass, and part of my ritual is to clean them. Your Grandpa Charlie has a footstone from the military showing he served in the Navy as a Lt. in World War II. On this visit, this good-sized, impressive marker was totally covered with thick, green, running grass and the engravings were filled with rich, dark mountain soil. It took me quite some time to clean it, kneeling on the grass, using my bare hands. When finished, I was pretty much adorned with dirt and grass. As I walked up to my car to get something to wipe myself off, another car pulled into the parking lot in front of the church. This was unusual, as it was mid-afternoon and the church was locked. Only once or twice in all my trips had I encountered other

11

people. As the couple approached me, we greeted one another; I asked of their family and they of mine. When I said "McCall", the lady asked which one and I replied that my Grandmother and Grandfather were Clyde Sebastian and Delphia Owen McCall. Immediately a soft smile of recognition appeared on her face. Then she spoke of my Grandmother, saying, "I knew Delphie. She came to church here every Sunday and was always so nice to me and the other children. I especially remember how every Sunday after services, she would walk down here to her husband's grave and visit for a long while." I hung on her every word, to me they were manna from heaven. I had been given a true story of my Grandmother which spoke to both her religious fidelity and her spiritual faithfulness.

I believe it was the same spiritual faithfulness which inspired her to keep a trunk filled with these letters, intact in their envelopes, for as long as she lived. Somehow she knew our spirits would need them someday. God bless her.

CHAPTER ONE

Life in Quebec

C harles Allen McCall, Sr., your Grandpa Charlie, was born in the midst of summer, July 20, 1919, in Quebec (pronounced *quee'-bec)*, Transylvania County, not far from where he is buried, in the pastorally beautiful Blue Ridge Mountains of Western North Carolina. He was the first-born child of Clyde Sebastian McCall and Delphia Omega Owen McCall. Clyde was seven years Delphia's senior; and according to family lore, was smitten with her when she was a mere child. He had to wait until she was sixteen to marry his long love. She was seventeen when Grandpa Charlie was born.

Your Grandpa Charlie's birth marked at least the sixth generation of Clyde Sebastian McCall's branch of the family tree to breathe this Carolina mountain air. Genealogical research reveals that immigrant members of the Scottish "McColl" clan crossed the Cumberland Gap with Daniel Boone. One of the most distinguished members of our clan in Scotland was Evan McColl, a Gaelic poet, born in 1808, at Kenmore on Loch Fyne, where a monument to his memory was erected in 1930. He authored "Clarsach nam Beann", translated "The Mountain Minstrel." Grandpa Charlie's Great-Great-Great Grandfather, Samuel McCall, was an itinerant wagon maker. In 1872, his son, John McCall, Sr., a Civil War veteran, bought a large portion of a sixty acre original land grant along Gloster Road and near the Blue Ridge Eastern Continental Divide. John, Jr. inherited the land from his father and ran a gristmill, which was powered by a small waterfall and used to make corn meal for his family and neighbors. The waterfall, known as "McCall Mill Shoals", is on the North Fork of Flat Creek in the Quebec community. John Jr's. son, Thomas Calhoun McCall, continued to run the mill and to provide corn meal to neighboring families for most of his life. His son, Clyde Sebastian McCall, was Grandpa Charlie's father and your great-grandfather. So, you can see that your own roots run deep in this incredibly beautiful land in the mountains, hills, and valleys of Western North Carolina.

Grandpa Clyde, who was the sixth child, had seven brothers; Wait, Till, Henry, Loon, Homer, Marvin, and Dee, and one sister, Canada who was the eldest. You will hear Uncle Loon referred to in these letters, he was a teacher. I have a faint memory of him; he and his wife, Aunt Viola, were always very nice to me. Their son, Cubby gave me my first puppy, a Christmas surprise, hidden in a box under the tree. Uncle Till ran a local country store, Uncle Marvin was Clerk of Court in Transylvania County for as long as I can remember him, and Uncle Henry farmed a large tract of land. Uncle Henry and Aunt Ola lived down below Grandpa Clyde and Grandma Delphie. When I was little, I would walk down toward their house with Grandma to get fresh spring water in a metal bucket, not a plastic bottle! The only thing I remember about Uncle Homer is that my little brothers, Allen and John, your fathers and uncles, called him "Oklahomer." Isn't it funny how we remember those little things? I don't know much about Wait and Dee or Canada. I do know Aunt "Cannie" (Canada McCall Young) lived to be eighty-three and is buried in the Oak Grove Baptist Cemetery adjacent to the graves of her parents, Thomas Calhoon and Pollyanna (Lydia P.) McCall. Aunt Cannie's eight "little brothers" (imagine that!) all lived to seventy and some into their late eighties, except for Grandpa Clyde who died at sixty-three of lung cancer. Yes, he was a smoker; in my memory he seemed to always be smoking a cigarette. Cascading down the hill from Thomas and Pollyanna's graves are those of Grandpa Clyde and Grandma Delphie, and on down those of Grandpa Charlie and Grandma Alice. My hope is that you will make a journey there sometime in your adult lives; it is a powerful experience to walk the land and graves of our ancestors. You will walk as members of the eighth generation of this McCall clan, a unique and rare opportunity which I encourage you to embrace.

Grandma Delphie and Grandpa Clyde had seven other children after Grandpa Charlie: Uncle John and Aunt Helen were close to his age; Aunt Sue, Uncle Jerry, Uncle Dan and Aunt Ducky (Ima Lee) were in the second group of children, and Uncle Joe Ben was the baby. Jerry, Dan and Joe Ben are the only surviving siblings. You will see references to each of them in the letters, particularly Uncle John who was a prisoner of war in Germany in WWII. You'll read "big brother" letters to his young siblings from Grandpa Charlie. You will find occasional scribbling of the children along with a few of Grandma Delphie's lists on some of the envelopes.

Uncle John, who I really don't remember, died from a gunshot wound in a hunting accident just after Christmas Day 1953. He was only thirty-one years old. According to our Aunt Sue, John had a sweet spirit. Michelle, your Daddy was named in honor of Uncle John. Aunt Helen moved to Baltimore, married Uncle Ed (Stockton) and raised their two daughters, Suzanne and Judy; she worked for the Social Security Administration until retirement. Helen was a wonderful seamstress and made a beautiful quilt of the family's life in Quebec which she brought once to a family reunion. Aunt Ducky also moved to Baltimore, married and raised her two daughters, Jennie and Katie. I have heard stories that after Ducky and Ed (Jenkins), a Catholic, were married, Grandma Delphie, a Southern Baptist, would not speak to her daughter for quite a while. (In my opinion, this is an excellent example of when religion may not be spiritual.) After they reconciled, I remember seeing Aunt Ducky and Uncle Ed coming home in an MG convertible, both in dark sunglasses, him in his spiffy driving cap, and Aunt Ducky with a scarf round her head flying like a flag as they rounded the curve toward Grandma's house. I thought that was the coolest thing I had ever seen! And, of course, most of you remember Aunt Sue. She married Uncle Carroll (Metcalf) and remained in Transylvania County to raise their two boys, Mike and Don; she worked at Belks Department Store for many years, and spent her last years in a senior living home on the outskirts of Brevard. She was my favorite: funny, smart, outspoken, a great cook, and full of family stories. One of the funniest things she ever said happened after we had all partaken of one of Grandma Delphie's wonderful meals. The family was all out on the front porch with the swing enjoying her homemade coconut cake, which was, as you would say, awesome! Grandma came out and asked my Daddy, Grandpa Charlie, if he wanted another piece of cake and then proceeded to ask the same of all her other "boys", John, Jerry, Dan and Joe Ben. I was just a little girl sitting next to Aunt Sue when I heard her say to her sisters and sisters-in-law, "We girls could all be starving to death and Mama would still be asking the boys if they wanted another helping!" A funny yet profound statement about the way things were in the South. I have often heard it said that if you want to know about your parents and family, ask your aunt. Remember that!

Grandpa Charlie's family home was built by his parents. It was a modest grayish frame country house, set on a hill at the end of a winding road and across from a beautiful horse pasture with a small lake. As you rounded the bend about a half mile away you would see the house; what an image of warmth and welcome it always was! I have often wondered what it must have been like for my father to round that bend and see his home place after returning from the horrors of war. I'm sure the family was on the front porch waving excitedly. From the mailbox on the winding country road, stones lead up the grassy hill to the weathered wooden front porch steps. Since there was no air conditioning, the porch was a place to relax and cool off, watch the occasional traffic go by, and visit with one another. You stepped through the front door into the small "front room" with a fireplace and modest seating. The old, dark wooden trunk was a focal point along with a piano and a small radio which was, excepting the newspaper, the only communication option of that era. I can see in my mind's eye all of the family gathered around the radio listening to an address by President Roosevelt. To the left of the front room was a bedroom with multiple iron beds with quilts Grandma Delphie had made. Just to the left of the fireplace was an opening leading to the dining room on the right where she fed her family around a picnic style wooden table with long benches on each side and a chair at either end. To the left of the dining room was another bedroom containing her and Grandpa Clyde's bed and another small bed built into the wall. Grandpa Clyde died in that room of lung cancer on Easter Sunday when he was only sixty-three. The only time I ever saw my Daddy cry was when he got a phone call telling him his father had died. He flew back from Oklahoma for the funeral by himself. When summer came, our family made the annual visit to North Carolina. I remember that when we went to Grandma Delphie's she must have sensed I was a little scared. I was only seven, and Grandpa's death was the first I had ever experienced. I have never forgotten how she put her plump, loving arm around me and took me into her room. As we stood there together looking at the bed where Grandpa died, she told me I didn't have to be afraid because every night when she went to bed she felt his arms go round her and she new everything was alright. In that moment, in that room, in that small house, this profoundly loving woman shaped my own spirituality forever. Beyond the dining room, across the back of the house was the kitchen which housed the big wood stove where Grandma Delphie cooked up her magic. Whether it was a "mess" of green beans, fried chicken, fried okra, corn-on-the-cob, fried squash, homemade biscuits (there was nothing else, thank God!), cornbread, apple pie, banana pudding or her famous coconut cake, it remains to this day the best food I have ever eaten. I remember not only the wonderful food, but her loving energy that went into preparing and serving these country meals. After she died in 1973, the most coveted of her possessions by her grandchildren was her Kool-Aid Pitcher. Her food and drink prepared in that kitchen were gifts to all of us. Off to the left of the kitchen was another small bedroom. There was no bathroom! Can you even imagine that? There was an outhouse up the hill and there were chamber pots in the bedrooms for the middle of the night. There was no running water. I already mentioned how she would gather spring water for drinking and cooking; and weekly Saturday night baths before Sunday church were taken in water gathered from rain barrels and heated on top of the wood stove. She didn't get indoor plumbing until I was well into my teenage years. When I look at the mega houses of today, I often wonder how much house is enough. This tiny home was enough for Grandma Delphie, Grandpa Clyde and their eight children. I never remember hearing her complain about being unhappy with her circumstances. She was, in fact, the most contented woman I have ever known. The property was sold not long after her death in 1973, but the house was not torn down until just a few years ago. The home site remains as it always was, undeveloped, and still full of the story and energy of the McCalls.

Grandpa Clyde was an interesting man. He was lanky and handsome with a hint of American Indian in his face (I've heard it said in a country way, not at all politically correct, that "there must have been an Indian in the woodpile.") I have no history on this, but I will say that Grandpa Charlie also had a Native American look about him, especially as he got older. If true, this only strengthens our bloodline and enriches our family story. Grandpa Clyde was a learned man, a school teacher who taught Grandpa Charlie, most of his other children and those of the community in a one-room school house. He wrote at the bottom of Grandpa Charlie's 7th grade report card on which he had given him high marks, "This is my own son's record and it is as near honest as can be. I have not given credit for his being who he is but rather what he is." I remember Aunt Sue telling me a few years before she died that she was no longer afraid because of a dream she had in which she was a little girl and her Daddy was carrying her over an icy bridge to school and she felt so safe and secure. He was, obviously, a good father. In addition to being a teacher, he was also a country Baptist preacher who preached at the Oak Grove Baptist Church among others. He baptized people in the river as depicted in the movie, *"Oh, Brother, Where Art Thou."* The music in his services must have been much like the sound track from that movie for there was always wonderful gospel singing on the front porch, around the piano in the front room and at our McCall family reunions. Incidentally, this was a pretty musical family; Uncle Jerry played the piano, Uncle Dan the guitar and most had great singing voices. Grandpa Clyde wasn't all teacher and preacher; he was also a practical joker. When I was a little girl, my Daddy and I were out in the yard with him and the chickens. (Yes, chickens, which provided eggs and Sunday dinners!) Grandpa asked me if I wanted to feed them, and, of course, I did. He handed me a burlap feed sack which I thought contained their food, but when I reached in my small hand grabbed a live chicken! Feathers flew and he and my Dad laughed so hard I couldn't help but laugh myself, after I stopped screaming!

Now a little more about Grandma Delphie's family: Her grandfather was John Dick Owen, and Irishman and an attorney; and one of his sons, her Uncle Jesse, was a minister. You will see references to him in some of Grandma Delphie's letters and read some of their correspondence to one another. Her father and mother were Paul Cub Owen and Elizabeth Gosnell about whom I have no other information; there are also few references to them in the letters. We do, however, find a clue about them in the somewhat creative and unique names they gave their ten offspring. In birth order they were, Eller, Carrie (who died of the flu at age 3), Roxie, Savannah, Beldora (who died at age twenty-four), Julius (who was a minister), Arletta (who died in infancy), Cornelious (who died at age eighteen), Vivian and the tenth and last child, our Grandmother, Delphia Omega. Naming their last born Delphia and Omega, (meaning, of course "the end"), two Greek names, certainly piques our curiosity. It is also quite a coincidence, Matt and McKenzie, that you are half Greek through your mother! Anyway, all the children whose deaths are not identified above lived into their late seventies and eighties, with Julius living longest to the age of eighty-eight. Of the children who survived beyond young adulthood, it was Grandma Delphie who died the earliest, at seventy-one of a heart attack. Thus, both she and Grandpa Clyde predeceased their mature siblings.

I remember our Grandmother as a short, very pleasant looking woman, with a kind, round face, soft blondish graying hair that was always curly and gently styled, and a semi-plump figure that was made for hugging. I don't recall her wearing anything but pretty cotton print dresses, but then I only saw her in the summertime. She made most of her own clothes and was particular about her appearance, always dressing up for Sunday services, I'm told. While to my knowledge she didn't sew, Aunt Sue inherited the desire for looking good; she had her hair "shampooed and set" every week, got permanents regularly, and always dressed in style. These traits of Southern female vanity still live on in some of us McCall girls! But Grandma Delphie was no "Southern Belle." She was a strong, workhorse of a woman. When she and Grandpa Clyde raised their family, you killed, plucked or skinned, dressed and cooked most all your meats. Vegetable were grown in the family garden and fruits and nuts came from local trees. It was a little like our farmers markets of today, but both the farm and the market were at their house. Planting, tending and harvesting the garden, gathering water, fruits and nuts, raising pigs, chickens and cows, as well as gathering the eggs and milking the cows, were just some of the routine chores. Of course, canning or "putting up" jams and jellies and vegetables for the winter was a must. Add to all of that the preparation of three meals a day on a wood stove which you had to load and fire up every time you cooked anything. No microwave! Maintenance to the property and house was done yourself as well. No Home Depot or Lowe's either! Grandma Delphie was the helpmate in these tasks while her husband was alive and managed many of them alone after he died. This was her land and she worked it with a passion. In addition to this she also raised her eight children sans maid, nanny or mother's morning out! I see her as one of the first "steel magnolias."

Hopefully, I have given you an adequate picture of life as Grandpa Charlie and his family knew it: rural, agricultural, family-centered, Southern Baptist, and poor. It is extremely significant to remember that in 1929, when Grandpa Charlie was barely ten years old, The Great Depression hit. Unemployment reached twenty-five percent, but rural communities were hurt the most, with crop and livestock prices falling as much as sixty — percent. Known as "Hard Times", these were difficult days in which to rear a large family. But Grandpa Charlie's parents managed to do a good job with him. Young Charles got good grades and lots of certificates for perfect attendance throughout his school days. He graduated valedictorian of the Rosman High School senior class of 1937. When he went off to College that fall, there were still six other children, most still very young, to be reared. The Depression began to moderate somewhat in the mid 1930's, but most of the recovery did not take place until the late 1930's and early 1940's, never totally ending until World War II.

There is also, of course, a family history and story on your Grandma Alice's, (Pettit) side of the family. All of you remember your Great Grandmother Lottie, *GiGi*, (Lottie Mae Norton Pettit). She and Granddaddy Pettit (Jennings Bryan Pettit) were also loving, good, hard-working people and were wonderful to me. Living in Brevard, they were my city grandparents. She was a nurse who at one time or another birthed and took care of most folks in Transylvania County; and he, a veteran of World War I, was a respected businessman and cobbler. He owned Pettit's Shoe Shop in Brevard and was easily recognizable driving his A-Model Ford around town, particularly on Wednesday afternoons, when all small town stores were closed. They also sent a son off to WWII, Uncle Bruce, who was one of the Air Force's renown "Flying Tigers". The story of the letters in *Delphie's Trunk* is a story of the McCalls, but is meant in no way to diminish the memory or legacy of the Pettits. You will find references to Grandma Alice and her family in the letters, and she actually penned some letters to Grandma Delphie. Perhaps one day the Pettit story will be told.

Thus far, I have told you in my own words and from my own perspective, some of our family history. Now my darlings, the letters, which begin over seventy years ago, in 1937, when Grandpa Charlie left home for the first time to attend Western Carolina Teachers College in Cullowhee, North Carolina. These are his own true words saved for a lifetime in an old trunk by his loving mother, Grandma Delphie.

Note: You will notice that the letters are addressed to Lake Toxaway, N.C. Quebec and Lake Toxaway are essentially the same community. The family referred to home as Quebec.

McCall Mill Shoals

STUDIES

REPO

NAME *Charles A. McCall* GRADE 7

Studies	1	2	3	4	5	6	7	8	9	Year
English Literature & Dramatization	A	A	A	a	a	a	a	a		88
Composition—Oral & Written	A	A	A	a	a	a	a	a		90
Spelling	A	A	A	a	a	a	a	a		99
Arithmetic	A-	A	A	a	a	a	a	a		86
History	A-	A	A	a	a	a	a	a		85
Geography and Nature Work	A	A	A	a	a	a	a	a		88
Reading	A	A	A	a	a	a	a	a		90
Phonics	A	A	A	a	a	a	a	a		90
Hygiene										
Writing	B	B+	B+	a	a	a	a	a		82
Drawing										
Music	A	A	A	a	a	a	a	a		90
Science										
Civics										
Physical Education	A	A	A	a	a	a	a	a		90
Times Present	20	20	20	20	20	20	20	20		160
Times Absent	0	0	0	0	0	0	0	0		0
Times Tardy	0	0	0	0	0	0	0	0		0
Conduct	A	A	A	a	a	a	a	a		G

EXPLANATION

"A"—indicates from 90-100   "C"—indicates from 70-79
"B"—indicates from 80-89   "D"—indicates below 70, unsatisfactory

Grade required for promotion is 70 or above

This is my own son's record and it is as near honest as can be. I have not given credit for his being who he is but rather what he is.

C. g. m.

The Senior Class of

Rosman High School

announce their

Commencement Exercises

May twentieth

nineteen hundred thirty-s

eight P. M.

High School Auditorium

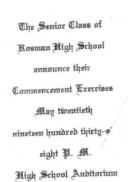

Charles McCall

CHAPTER TWO

Cullowhee Student and Grover Teacher

The brief letters and postcards in this Chapter are a prelude to the full body of letters your Grandpa Charlie wrote while in the Navy during World War II. Through these letters from Cullowhee, N.C., you will get a feeling for the innocence and promise of his college days at Western Carolina Teachers College. I transcribed the letters in this book exactly as my Daddy wrote them, including all spelling and grammatical errors found on the originals. This verbatim approach not only shows us Grandpa Charlie's humanity, but also accurately represents the education and maturation process he experienced over the years of this correspondence. It is now October of 1937 and young Charles McCall pens his first letter to his parents.

Western Carolina Teachers College
Cullowhee, North Carolina
January 11, 1937

OFFICE OF THE BURSAR

Mr. Charles McCall
Lake Toxaway
North Carolina

Dear Mr. McCall:

This is to acknowledge receipt of two dollars for room reservation for the fall quarter, 1937, together with your application for work. We are enclosing receipt for same. We shall be glad to give you a room with Mr. Tinsley just as soon as he sends in his reservation fee.

We are filing your application for work. Please have at least three prominent people write us as to your ability, need, and worthiness. You will find enclosed a high school transcript blank, which is to be filled out by your principal and returned to the Registrar as promptly as possible. We cannot tell you definitely about the work until we know whether we shall receive NYA aid again this year. We are usually notified about August 1.

We are looking forward to having you with us, and we will be glad to help you in any way we can.

Very truly yours,

Ruth Oliver Hinds,
Bursar

MLB

Enclosures 2

WESTERN CAROLINA
TEACHERS COLLEGE
Cullowhee, N.C.

Sunday evening
(October 4, 1937)

Dear Folks;

How are you all? I'm getting along fine, having to study awful hard. Things over here are lots different from High School, it takes about three hours of study to prepare for a one hour class. We sometimes have to report on a whole library book for one class. I think I'll make it allright though. English is the hardest subject I have to write themes and make talks, and they have to be just about perfect.

I went to church this morning and was planning to go hunt some chestnuts this evening but its raining and I don't have anything special to do.

We have a boxing exhibition next Friday night, Julius and I are matched. There will be about twelve fights of three rounds each.

I don't know now just when I'll get to come home but will let you know.

Tell John to answer the card I wrote. All of you write.

Sincerely yours,
Chas.

Cullowhee, N. C.

Sunday evening

Dear Folks;

How are you all? I'm getting along fine, having to study awful hard. Things over here are lots different from High School, it takes about three hours of study to prepare for a one hour class. We sometimes have to report on a whole library book for one class. I think I'll make it allright though. English is the hardest subject I have, we have to write themes and make talks, and they have to be just about perfect.

I went to church this morning and was planning to go hunt some chestnuts this evening but its raining and I don't have anything special to do.

We have a boxing exhibition next Friday night, Julius and I are matched. There will be about twelve fights of three rounds each.

I don't know now just when I'll get to come home but will let you know.

Tell John to answer the card I wrote. All if you write.

Sincerely yours
Chas.

Cullowhee, N.C.
October 10, 1937

Dear Mama,

I got your letter and the apples. I was glad to get them both, we had been out of apples for two or three days and those were sure good.

I'm getting along fine, except for my eyes. They have been giving me some trouble, but are getting better now. I guess it's because I've not read any in so long.

I went to church this morning and to-night. This morning there was a girl from Brazil, a girl from Russia, and a converted Jew (boy) who all talked to us, the Jew preached. The girl from Russia made the most interesting talk. She told how the communists destroyed her fathers property, because he was wealthy, and how they hid at day and traveled at night (walking) until they got to China. She left her parents and came to America and didn't hear from them for two years. She also sang a song in Russian then in English. She cannot speak English very well.

We don't have any school next Saturday so I guess I'll come home Friday. I don't know just what time I can get off but I'll get a way home.

Tell Ducky that her letter was very interesting but that she should know better how to divide her subject matter into paragraphs and that each paragraph should have a topic sentence.

Tell John that if he don't answer my card with a letter that I'll never write him again. Tell Helen and Sue both to write me. A letter ever now and then sure does come in good.

William D. Upshaw made an awfully interesting talk over here last week. He is going to send me a book because I was first to answer a question that he asked according to parliamentary law. He represented preacher Summey's "painted up girls as counterfeit, representing something that they are not.

Well its ten o'clock, bed time so answer soon. Guess I'll see you all Friday evening or Friday night.

Love   (P.S.)

Chas.   over—

Monday Night

Since I wrote this I have found out that the road by way of Glenville is closed and that I have classes until four o'clock Friday so I don't know when I'll come home. I guess I'll come Sat. but don't look for me if I don't come.

Chas.

Cullowhee, N. C.
October 22, 1937

Dear Folks;

I would have wrote sooner but, as I suppose you know, Julius went home Tuesday and was coming back Wednesday and I told him to bring John back with him. He got home too late and didn't get to see him.

I'm left in the room by myself. Several boys want to move in and some want me to move in with them but I think I'll stay by myself. I can study better and don't have anyone to bother me.

Julius took all his things and left me in pretty bad shape. I didn't have a razor or comb, but I bought a comb and some other things and am buying razor blades for another boy and using his razor.

I don't know what made Julius leave, I recon he "just couldn't take it." I'm getting along fine and liking better every day.

We are having Homecoming day on November 6 (Saturday) and I've been asked to invite you all over. We have a program in the morning and a football game in the evening. It will be a big day so come if you can. Your dinners will cost you twenty five cents each.

It has rained over here every day this week until yesterday and is raining again to-day. It's kind of troublesome about going to meals and classes.

Well, its about time for class so I'll have to close. All of you write to me.

Love,
Charles

Cullowhee, N.C.
Oct. 30, 1937

Dear Daddy;

I was very glad to get your letter and the money. I was needing the money pretty bad and the letter also was a great help.

I got Helen's box and the paper last night and was very glad to get them. The cake is real good, and thanks to John for the apples and pears.

Come over for the Homecoming if you can, at least you and John come. I imagine that Mama would have a rather hard time with the babies, not having any place to keep them.

I got a letter from Julius last week wanting me to find out if he could come back. They told me that he could if he would come by Thursday. I wrote him but he didn't show up. He seems to have a good bit of trouble "finding himself." I'm getting along just as good without him.

My letters may seem short but really there's little more I can say than I'm getting along fine.

All of you write and tell me the news, I'm always extremely glad to hear.

Love,
Charles

WESTERN CAROLINA
TEACHERS COLLEGE
Cullowhee, N. C.

November, 21, 1937

Dear Folks;

I got mama's letter and the papers yesterday. I'm glad you sent the pathfinder, I'm expected to keep up with world news and its hard to read the whole news paper every day.

I'm getting along just fine and having a good time. It's been awfully cold over here for the last two or three days, the river was frozen over this morning.

I suppose you all went to Cashiers to-day. I went to Sunday School and Church this morning. Mr. Elliott is my Sunday School teacher and I enjoy hearing him. Where are Daddy and Gene holding the revival? Is Gene staying there?

Well, its just four weeks until Christmas Holidays and if I can stand a week of examination I will be 1/12 through college. It seems like a long time, yet time flys over here. I will have all my work for this quarter in next Saturday then I will have more time to study. I don't suppose I will come home until Christmas because I will have so much studying to do.

Answer soon and tell me about everybody.

Love,
Chas.

Cullowhee, N. C.
Nov. 30, 1937

Dear Mama;

I got your letter to-day, was glad to hear from you. I'm getting along all right, having to study hard for examinations. I have one final examination to-morrow and one Saturday.

I moved to-day. One of the Instructers is getting married and they are moving one that is not married into my room so that The man and his wife can move into one of the two roomed suites. I am on third floor now in 309.

I saw Clarence McCall and Mary Jane last Sunday. Four of us boys walked down to the monument for "Aunt Sally" where John R. Brinkley was borned and they passed us at East la Porte.

I read about Mr. Henderson's death in the Ashville paper the morning after he died. I said something to Truette about it the next morning and he didn't know it.

I hate to say it but I will need about $2.50 to settle some accounts before Christmas. We take memographed tests and have to pay for them and I owe some on a Library book I kept overtime. I borrowed .50 to pay for a work-book last week.

Tell Gene that I'm expecting him to be there Christmas and that I want him to go hunting with me.

I went rabbit hunting and ate dinner with a Ferguson man that lives here in the community Thanksgiving day. I didn't have Turkey but did have chicken and dumplings, sweet potatoes and butter, and home made molasses and hot biscuits.

I'm through working this quarter. About 300 tons of coal in the coal bin started burning (by sponetanous combustion) last Saturday night and I, with about 25 other boys worked until twelve o'clock moving it out with shovels and wheelbarrows.

Rosman was supposed to have played Cullowhee High School at basketball here tonight. I went down but they didn't come.

If nothing happens I'll be coming home two weeks from Friday evening about four o'clock.

Answer soon and tell me the news.

Love,
Charles

Cullowhee, N. C.
December 8, 1937

Dear Mama;

I received your and John's letter yesterday. I was glad to hear from both of you and to get the money, I needed it very badly. I am going to register to-day for the next quarter, since I am working they are giving me until December 21 to pay. If I wait until after then it will cost me five dollars late registration fee. Last year they didn't register until after the Holidays but they have changed it this year. I won't have to buy but one book for next quarter and I guess about $45 will pay for everything. I will know exactly how much it will take, today after I register.

I have had all my final tests but two. I made the highest grade in Geography and several Juniors and Seniors were in the class with me. My term paper counts as my final test in English and I'm handing it in to-day. That only leaves Algebra and History and I don't dread either of them at all.

I'm sorry you all have colds. I have a slight one but am feeling just fine, I has been awfully cold over here for two or three days. The river froze over last night and the lights went out about 9 o'clock.

I guess you all will have to come after me on ether Friday after four o'clock or sometime Saturday. I had rather you would wait until Saturday if it will be satisfactory, it will give me time to get my things ready.

Tell John that I will answer his letter to-night.

Love,
Chas.

Cullowhee, N.C.
January 17, 1937
(actually 1938)

Dear Daddy,

Hope you are having a happy birthday.

I'm getting along fine except for a slight cold I began taking this morning.

I was glad to get the papers and the letter.

I suppose I will come home a week from Saturday but you needn't come after me.

Tell Ducky that I will answer her letter soon.

I have a class in three minutes so I will have to close. Answer soon.

Love,
Chas.

Cullowhee, N.C.
January 17, 1937

Dear Daddy;

Hope you are having a
happy birthday.

I'm getting along fine
except for a slight cold I began
taking this morning.

I was glad to get the
papers and the letter.

I suppose I will come
home a week from Saturday
but you needn't come after me.

Tell Ducky that I will
answer her letter soon.

I have a class in three
minutes so I will have to close.
Answer soon

Love,
Chas

Cullowhee, N.C.
January 23, 1938

Dear Mama,

I got your letter with Stamps and cards. You guessed about right, I am a little scarce of money. I borrowed $1.00 last week to have my picture made for the College Annual. I'll make it all right, though, until I come home Saturday.

I hope you all are getting along fine. I'm first rate.

It's an awfully pretty day and I think I'll take to the woods. I know where there is a walnut tree that has lots of walnuts under it, it's about five miles to it but I guess I'll head that way.

I had a card from Ralph Owen last week, a letter from Julius and got the papers last night.

If you have time I wish that you would put some kind of old half-sole on those shoes I left. The old ones I work in are about off my feet.

Tell John and Helen to write me, and you answer soon.

Love,
Chas.

DEAR DUCKY:

HOW ARE YOU? ARE YOU WORKING HARD? DON'T WORK TOO HARD. WHEN HAVE YOU BEEN TO TOXAWAY OR CASHIERS? TELL JERRY HELLO AND SEE IF HE CAN READ THIS: Q. ANSWER REAL SOON.

WITH LOVE,
CHARLES

P.S. I AM COMING HOME NEXT SATURDAY.

me, and you answer soon.

Your,
Chas.

DEAR DUCKY:

HOW ARE YOU? ARE YOU WORKING HARD?
DON'T WORK TOO HARD. WHEN HAVE YOU
BEEN TO TOXAWAY OR CASHIERS? TELL
JERRY HELLO AND SEE IF HE CAN READ
THIS: Q. ANSWER REAL SOON

WITH LOVE,
CHARLES

P.S. I AM COMING HOME NEXT SATURDAY.

Cullowhee, N.C.
February 6, 1938

Dear Mama,

I got your card and was glad to hear from you. I also got the paper last night.

I'm getting along fine. I have mid-term examinations this week and have been studying pretty hard.

I got here Monday morning about ten o'clock, missed one class.

Bud, Elsie, and Margaret White and Paul Whitmire were over here last night. We had a basketball game, played Fort Braig.

How is everything going at home? I hope you are all well.

I had a letter from Helen Henderson this week. She told me a good bit of the news.

I have to buy a Science Work-book this week which costs seventy five cents. Daddy gave me $3.00 but I owed $1.50 and it cost me .50 to come over here. I got a haircut, went to the senior play which cost me .25 and bought some more things I needed and I only have about .20. If you all have the difference I wish you would send it.

Love,
Chas

(February 2, 1938)

Dear Mama,

Can't come in this Sunday. Going to Rosman Thursday, will come by to see you then.

I am getting along O.K. Hope you folks are.

Love,
Chas.

2/21/38

Dear Folks:

I am getting along O.K. Hope you all are too.

Julius, Frank, and Leo Reid were over to see me yesterday. I kind of wanted to go back with them but couldn't. I suppose I will be home this week-end, one of the boys may come with me, I'll let you know later if he is going too.

I got the paper Sat. night.

Answer soon
Chas.

3/7/38

Dear Mama,

I was glad to get your card and the paper.

I'm getting along fine, will get through my work to-day and will have to go to studying most of the time, getting ready for tests. I will need about a dollar to pay for my examination books and memographs.

Were you all at Grandpa's? I saw the article in the paper.

I will be ready to come home Friday 18, at four o'clock or Saturday.

Answer
Chas.

4/20/38

Dear Folks;

I hope you all are well. I am fine. I have just been elected to the W.C.T.C. Senate, the highest honor a Freshman can hope for. Four candidates were nominated by the Freshman class and then voted on by the whole student body. I will serve all next year and get a free weeks trip to some resort for a pre-session conference just before it begins.

Answer soon,

Love
Chas.

(October 17, 1938)
Wed.

Dear Folks;

I am getting along fine. The boy came after me Sunday and I made it O.K.

I have a chance to buy a good straight razor for $1.00. I believe it is a bargain if you were to allow me that much.

Hope some of you can come over Saturday.

Write me soon.

Chas.

(November 2, 1938)

Dear Mama,

George Hannah is coming home with me and we will be there sometime Friday evening or Friday night.

Don't go to much trouble fixing up for him because he is just a plain boy.

We may come with the mail or may hitch-hike.

Answer and tell me the news.

Love,
Chas.

(November 12, 1938)
Wednesday

Dear Folks,

I'm getting along fine. I got the letter and paper Monday.

George and I are coming Nov. 18 instead of Thanksgiving.

I don't know of anything interesting to write now. Hope to hear from you all soon.

Love,
Chas.

(Nov. 21, 1938)

Hello Friends;

Here is a word of cheer for the big happy family. How is every one these cold days? This is fine weather for my work, but you know I smyphathise with the folks back home who has some work that must be done after school these cold days.

Here is my thanks for the nice time I had. I was really home sick when I came back to school. It seemed like being at home. I will add that I rather be at your home than any place I have ever been.

Tell all the children that old Santa will soon be over that way.

Charles is getting along very nicely. He sure is a fine fellow. He is also working good, too.

George

(Boone, N.C.
Feb. 3, 1939)

Hey Folks,

I am at Boone having a nice time and debating once about every two hours.

Will write more when I get back.

(Cullowhee, N.C.
Feb. 25, 1939)

Tues.

Dear Mama,

I am O.K. Hope you are well. I hope you can send me some money by tomorrow, or I stop eating.

I will come home one week from Friday if I can get there. I am going home with Max this weekend.

Write me soon.

Love
Chas.

Cullowhee, N.C.
March 30, 1939

Dear Daddy,

I am leaving today for the University of North Carolina to the Southern Conference of Student government associations. I need a little money, but it is too late now. I have been expecting you to send me some, or write me since Tuesday. I wonder what is wrong.

I will get back Sunday night and will write more then.

Sincerely,
Chas. A. McCall

(Williamsburg, V.A.
Apr. 6, 1939)

Hey Folks,

I am at Williamsburg having a nice time. Spent Wed. night in Winston Salem, got there in the afternoon. Going to Jamestown & Yorktown now and probably to Washington tomorrow.

Chas.

(Raleigh, N.C.
Oct. 27, 1939)

Thu. Night

Dear Mama,

I am having a nice time inspecting the Capitol city. I ate lunch today at the table next to where the Gov. was eating.

I will introduce my bill tomorrow afternoon. Write me soon.

Love,
Charles

(Cullowhee, N.C.
Nov. 27, 1939)

Monday

Dear Mama,

I got the paper and the letter. Will save the clipping for you. The pictures are good. I had to pay three cents to get them.

I am badly in need of $2.00 for club dues and supplies. Hope it will be possible for you to send it.

I have to register Dec. 6 and will need some money then, and it isn't long off.

I am going to Mars Hill Tomorrow to Debate.

Answer Soon,

Chas.

Monday

Dear Mama,

I got the paper and the letter.
Will save the clipping for you.
The pictures are good. I had to pay
three cents to get them.

I am badly in need of $2.00
for club dues and supplies. Hope
it will be possible for you to
send it.

I have to register Dec. 6
and will need some money then,
and it isn't long off.

I am going to Mars Hill
tomorrow to debate.

Answer soon.
Chas

Mrs. Clyde

COUILLOW
NOV 27
4 PM
1939
N.C.

(Rock Hill, N.C.
Dec. 7, 1939)

Dear Mama,

I am having a nice time down here and speaking lots.

I wanted to come by to see you as we came by but didn't have time. Will see you soon.

Love,
Charles

WESTERN CAROLINA
TEACHERS COLLEGE
Cullowhee, North Carolina

Jan. 2, 1940

Dear Mama,

I promised to write you from Tennessee, but the post office was closed when I got there Saturday and you know yesterday was New Years Day and it was closed again.

I had a very good trip and got back yesterday afternoon.

I got my overcoat at the Peoples Store. I had to pay $24.50 for it, but Helen said for me to get a good one and she would take care of the payments. The monthly payments will be raised to $6.00 instead of $4.00.

I hope you are all well. I feel fine and am ready to begin studying.

I suppose you got my grades.

Love,
Chas.

(Cullowhee, N.C.
January 5, 1940)

Sunday

Dear Mama,

I am getting along O.K. I haven't written because I haven't had postage. I need a little money pretty bad for a haircut and some things. I will make out until you get some. Helen hasn't sent the reservation money yet.

It has been terribly cold over here for the last few days. I suppose you saw in the paper that our temperature was—17 one morning. It has been down around—15 every morning since then. It is bad about going to early classes. Since I am on the Deans Honor roll, I don't have to attend classes except when I want to and I have been sleeping late these mornings.

Burke and I are coming over to spend the night before long. I am going to speak at Rosman High School chapel one day and we will come over the night before. I don't know the exact date, but it will be sometime within the next month. Max and I may come over one week-end before then.

I hope the weather opens up so Daddy's school can start. Tell Ducky, Jerry and Dan Hello for me, and that I will be over to see them before long.

Love Always,
Chas. A.

(The board will Be O.K.)

WESTERN CAROLINA TEACHERS COLLEGE
Cullowhee, North Carolina

TO THE PARENTS OR GUARDIANS:

This is to advise that ___Charles McCall___ has been reported at the
mid-term of the ___Winter___ quarter as doing the quality of work as indicated by
check (X) below:

SUBJECTS	SATISFACTORY	POOR	FAILING	COMMENTS
Eng. 235				
Phys. 342	✓			
Ed. 331H	✓			
Math. 332	✓			
Phys. 342	✓			
Hyg. 331				
P.E. 317a				

Parents and guardians will please understand that these checks do not indicate final
grades for the quarter. They simply show how the student is standing with reference
to his various subjects at mid-term. And just as a subject checked poor or failing
at mid-term may be changed by the student's effort to a satisfactory grade by the
end of the quarter, so it is possible for a satisfactory check at mid-term to become
poor or failing by the end of the quarter. Any cooperation, therefore, on the part
of parents or guardians to encourage students to maintain a satisfactory quality of
work or to overcome handicaps and difficulties is not only welcomed but earnestly
solicited by the college faculty.

___2/17/40___   (S) ___Archie Beam___
Date   Registrar

(Chapel Hill, N.C.
Mar. 31, 1940)

Saturday night

Dear Mama,

Our convention ended tonight and I am leaving here in the morning.

I have had a good time and learned a lot.

Hope to see you folks next Saturday if I can get home.

Love,
Chas. A.

(Cullowhee, N.C.
Apr. 15, 1940)

Sunday

Dear Folks,

I hope you are all well. I am O.K. The weather is rather cold over here now, it doesn't seem like we are going to have any summer.

I am in need of some money now, more that I should ask for I guess, but it seems that I must have some. I have to pay $3.00 as Junior Class dues for the banquet, $1.00 for a class, and $2.25 for a book. I hope you will be able to send it.

If you still get the Brevard paper, I would like for you to send it over now and then, I like to keep up with politics over there. Burke is running for the Legislature in Jackson, on the wrong side, of course, to be elected.

Mr. Ferguson's father is seriously ill, and they are spending most of their time over there, so I don't know whether it will be advisible to come next Sunday or not. I will let you know later.

Yours,
Chas. McCall

HEADS STUDENTS — Charles McCall (above) of Lake Toxaway, in Transylvania county, was elected president of the student body of Western Carolina Teachers college at Cullowhee in balloting this week. He is a senior, president of the International Relations club, inter-collegiate debater and representatives to the student legislature. He was designated the best college citizen last year and has served for three years in the student senate.

(Raleigh, N.C.
Oct. 27, 1940)

Sunday

Dear Mama,

Been here since Thursday, leaving now for Cullowhee. Write more later.

Yours,
Chas.

(Rock Hill, N.C.
Dec. 6, 1940)

Thursday night

Dear Mama,

I am here at Rock Hill debating. Will be here until Sunday.

Hope you are all well. Let me hear from you.

Yours,
Chas. A.

(Cullowhee, N.C.
May 28, 1941)

Wednesday

Dear Mama,

Sorry to have missed you Sunday. Hope you are all well.

Must have $12.00 by Saturday by some hook or crook.

Let me hear from you.

Charles

Wednesday

Dear Mama,

Sorry to have missed you Sunday.
Hope you are all well.

Must have $12.00 by Saturday by
some hook or crook.

Let me hear from you.

Charles

THIS SIDE OF CARD IS FOR ADDRESS

Mrs. Clyde S. McCall
Lake Toxaway,
N. C.

The Faculty and

Class of Nineteen Hundred Forty-one

Western Carolina Teachers College

request the honor of your presence

at the

Commencement Exercises

on Monday morning, June ninth

at ten o'clock

Clyde R. Hoey Auditorium

Grover, N.C.
July 27, 1941

Dear Mama,

I got here O.K. Had a little trouble getting located since it was two o'clock when I arrived and didn't know exactly where to go.

I have a nice place to stay, the people are nice and I like it fine—everything except the heat and it is terrible. The days don't seem much hotter than up there but the nights are as hot or hotter than the days. I can't do a thing but sit and sweat until after twelve o'clock. I hope I will get used to it before long.

I would like for you to look through my things and send me the leather brief case, a class roll book, my brown shoes, the old brown pants, the red, white and blue shirt, and my books.

This is a nice little town between the size of Rosman and Brevard. It is on the main line of the Southern Railway and there is a train through every thirty minutes, day and night. Two deisil streamliners come through at 7 and 11. That don't help put me to sleep either.

Five girl teachers stay here where I do and I am the only man. I am the only single man in the whole faculty of 18 most of whom are single girls so I think I will do right well (don't tell Daddy).

Let me know how you are all getting along. Have my mail forwarded, please.

Much Love,
Charles

Grover, N.C.
September 16, 1941

Dear Mama,

Your card and the paper came Sunday. Glad to hear that you are all O.K. How is Helen now? Let me know how she is getting along.

I think School will be out here Friday. I haven't decided yet just what I will do then. They want me to come back and teach until Christmas and have offered me a job here in a store during the time school is out. I think, however, that I will go to Norfolk but will come by home if possible. I suppose I will ship my things home the last of the week so if I shouldn't get home look after them for me.

We are giving our play Friday night and it is keeping me busy now. School has been turning out at twelve thirty every day and I have been working on stage scenery from then until supper time. We practice every night from eight until eleven thirty.

I am not going to write to you another time until I get a letter. I am tired of postal cards. Let me hear from you often and don't disappoint me with just a card. Tell everyone hello for me.

Love,
Charles

How different Grandpa Charlie's college experience was from that of today. There was no Facebook, texting, e-mail, cell phone or even telephone; all personal communication was by the mail, delivered along rural roads by postmen driving a vehicle you could hitch a ride on. Matt and McKenzie, I'm sure you can relate to being in college and asking your parents for money, but could you believe the price of things? The senior play cost him twenty-five cents and was the only entertainment expense of the letters. There was no mall, movie theater, corner hangout, club, television, or internet. Other than school activities, church was the sole source of interesting, communal activity. In the South, church remains to this day the center of social life for many people. Walking five miles and back to gather walnuts was how Grandpa Charlie spent a Sunday afternoon. It's hard to even imagine the quiet peaceful solitude he must have known on that walk.

Many years before reading these letters, while exploring the contents of the trunk, I learned from old newspaper clippings and his collection of lapel pins that Grandpa Charlie was a college honor student and had been president of the Western Carolina Student Senate. However, I learned for the first time from these letters that he was an accomplished debater. He never spoke of this to me, but I do remember that he was keenly interested in politics and world events. When I was growing up, we had one television, and I hated how Daddy always wanted to watch the news at dinner time when I had something more entertaining in mind. The news always prevailed, and Daddy never missed the live broadcasts of the Democratic Conventions. By the way, we did not get our first television until I was seven. Before that I would have to go next door to watch, *Howdy Doody*, my favorite program and one of the only shows broadcast at that time. I also remember how much Grandpa Charlie loved to watch boxing, but I never knew until now he was boxer. How quiet he was about himself!

Did you notice how much Grandpa Charlie wrote about his studies and that even in college his grades, including mid-terms, were sent to his parents? Good grades remained of paramount importance to him when he became a father.

Grandpa Charlie's working for a coal supplier during college was also news to me. That must have been very hard work. Between that, all the walking and boxing, he must have been in great physical shape. Throughout all of this life and personal struggles, a strong work ethic remained a cornerstone of my Father's character.

These letters consistently reveal Grandpa Charlie's keen interest in and concern for his family, which only grows stronger the more he is separated from them by life and war. He would be very pleased to know that we continue this tradition of staying in touch with family. Lately a saying of Grandma Delphie's has been on my mind, "I've been so hungry to see you!" This simple phrase expresses so well our primal need to stay connected, to reach out to one another and be fed.

Grandpa Charlie graduated from Western Carolina Teachers College June 8, 1941, earning a Bachelor of Science Degree in Education, with a major in Mathematics and a Minor in Science. There is no GPA on his transcript, but interestingly, he made mostly B's with A's and C's competing for second place. He took the required courses you would expect and some of the most interesting of those and his electives were: Math & Civilization, Fencing, Vocational Guidance, Old Testament History, Football Coaching, Buying and Budgeting, Current Social Problems, Contemporary European History, and Salesmanship. With his degree in education, Grandpa Charlie took a teaching job in Grover, North Carolina. Life there was hot, both in climate and company; out of a faculty of eighteen, mostly female, he was the only single male! And he lived in a boarding house with five of the girls. Of course, in those days the environment in a boarding house was very prim and proper; wonder how he got around that? From the sound of his few letters from Grover, he was a very dedicated and involved teacher, even directing and building sets for a student play. As the rest of the letters unfold you will read about more of the cultural experiences and interests of your Grandpa Charlie.

Isn't it strange how we think we know our parents and grandparents, but we only know them from the perspective of being their children. We forget they lived a whole chunk of life as a child and young adult before we ever came along. To us they are grownups, almost larger than life, but in reality they were once young and vulnerable like we were. Rarely do we get an opportunity to travel back in time and see what our parents' early lives were like, but that is exactly what these letters invite us to do. Megan, I am reminded of when you were a little girl and the times we took you to Lenox Square Mall. You would stand with your wide-eyed, tiny little face pressed up against the Disney Store display window and say, "I want in there!" So let us continue through our window filled with antique letters onto the next phase of Grandpa Charlie's life.

CHAPTER THREE

Naval Enlistment and Newport News

World War II began on September 1, 1939, when Nazi Germany, under the leadership of fascist dictator Adolf Hitler, invaded Poland. As a result Britain and France immediately declared war against Germany. Grandpa Charlie was just beginning his junior year of college. The war spread like a cancer across the globe. Italy, also ruled by a fascist dictator, Benito Mussolini, joined with Germany to form the primary Axis forces of WWII. France fell to German & Italian forces in June of 1940, and was divided between and occupied by these armies for over four years. Having already invaded China in 1937, and attempting to invade Russia, Japan joined with Germany and Italy in September of 1940, to become the third major power on the Axis side. All three Axis powers were driven by a nationalistic obsession to exercise militaristic power over the world and totally eliminate democracy. In spite of the aggression of the Axis forces, public opinion in our country was heavily against American involvement. Until the Japanese bombing of Pearl Harbor on December 7, 1941, the United States, under the leadership of President Franklin Delano Roosevelt (FDR), maintained a policy of neutrality.

Charles Allen McCall, Sr. enlisted in the Navy on August 18, 1941, at the Charlotte, N.C. recruiting station. His "Report of Physical Examination" showed him to be a healthy twenty-two year old (your age Megan), and with the exception of pneumonia at age 3 with no complications, showed him to have no personal or family history of illness. He was a scrapping 150 lbs. and 71 ½ inches tall, with a chest measurement of 33" at expiration and 38" at inspiration and a 31" waist. Notes reflect that he had lost about 10 lbs the past 3 weeks playing basketball. His blue eyes had perfect 20/20 vision. He had blood pressure of 128/70 both sitting and standing. The records also show he had been vaccinated for Smallpox in 1928 and for Typhoid in 1940, and had experienced no injuries or operations. Grandpa Charlie was a healthy young mountain man!

His orders on that August day were to USNR, Class V-7 for engineering duties. He was to proceed to his home and follow his usual civilian occupation until he received orders from the Bureau of Navigation to report to school, expected to be sometime in January 1942. As a member of the Navy Reserve he was to keep the Bureau of Navigation advised of his address at all times. It was suggested that he read all the recommended engineering books before reporting for duty.

On December 9, 1941, Grandpa Charlie was sent a five page letter addressed to: CANDIDATES FOR RESERVE MIDSHIPMAN'S SCHOOL, U.S. NAVAL ACADEMY, stating that he was to report to the Academy on January 9, 1942, for enrollment as a "Prospective Reserve Midshipman." Most of the letter consisted of a long and extensive list of instructions and required personal items. Logan, it reminds me a lot of your materials for AMERICORP. Some of the items he was to bring were: bathrobe; bedroom slippers; nail, hair, shaving and tooth brushes; cufflinks; garters; white handkerchiefs; stationery and a whisk broom. Regarding cars the instructions were: "Reserve Midshipmen are permitted to ride in automobiles in company with Officers and Instructors *only*. You will not be permitted to drive automobiles." Grandpa Charlie was instructed to arrive with $10.00 cash, as opposed to your $200, Logan! The letter ended in part, "During the first month of your course you will be designated and referred to as Prospective Reserve Midshipman. This period will be devoted primarily to Executive (military) drills, lectures, and inspections; Physical Training; Practical Ordinance drills, and Seamanship Lectures . . . . Candidates failing to pass physical requirements and those considered unsatisfactory in 'Aptitude for the Service' will be dropped from the school . . . . The second part of the course will be . . . two terms of six weeks of Academic 'Engineer School.' . . . you will receive instruction in Marine and Electric Engineering and continue drills . . . and Department Physical Training." The last paragraph began, "The course of training will be intensive and in parts, difficult and exacting."; and ended, "We feel sure that the patriotic urge that prompted you to apply for this opportunity will stand you in good stead in your efforts to measure up to the high standards of honor, loyalty, obedience, and proficiency that will be required of you throughout the course."

In October 1941, your Grandpa Charlie set out for Newport News, Virginia to work in the Naval Shipyards while awaiting orders to Annapolis. Once again, in his own true words, the story continues.

(written on his WNC Student Senate stationery
October, 1941)

Mama,

I'm going to Brevard to spend the night so I'll have a good start in the morning. With good luck I'll make it by tomorrow night sometime, otherwise I may have to spend the night somewhere. Will let you hear from me as soon as I get there.

Until further notice my address will be

> 326—43rd Street
> Newport News, Va.
> c/o George H. Hannah

Forward my mail to that address with this exception: If I get any mail from the Navy Department open it and read it. If it is an order for me to report to duty soon, send me a wire telling me when and where. Be sure to do that because the notice is not sent more than four or five days beforehand.

I think I am taking everything I need but may have to send for something before long. I'm sure I'll need my overcoat but will let you know when to send it.

If everything turns out as I have planned I'll be back about Christmas time. If not, I might be back in a couple of weeks. Until then, Good-bye and good luck,

Charles

326—43rd Street
Newport News, Va.
(OCT 22, 1941)
(postcard)

Dear Mama,

I had very good luck coming up. I got to Danville,
Va. Monday night and here about two o'clock yesterday.

I think I will start to work tomorrow. I'm staying with George at
present.

I would like for you to mail my last year's annual to me. George
wants to see it.

Let me hear from you soon.

Love,
Charles

(October 26, 1941)

326—43ʳᵈ Street
Newport News, Va.
Sunday

Dear Daddy,

I received the letter and card. Thanks a lot for your offer to assist but I think it will be O.K. There was a misunderstanding that I have cleared up I think. The bank was to renew the balance of my note for 60 days and they haven't done it.

I have been working two days now. I am in the arc welding class here at the Shipyard. They are paying me thirty five dollars a week until I learn which should be about four weeks and after that time I will get $1.25 per hour plus time and half time all day Saturday. I could have had a time keeping job but that would have only paid me thirty two dollars per week straight. I am making more money welding and learning a valuable trade in addition. I work six days per week from 4 until 12 o'clock.

Living expenses are rather high. Board is $8.00 per week and other things in proportion. Even at that, however, I am making more than I did teaching. Let me hear all the news.

Yours,
Charles

(Grandma Delphie's note on a Selective Service letter to Grandpa Charlie)

October 28, 1941

Charles, if I had time I'd write a letter. But Mr. Thomas *is waiting on me. I got your letter just now. Will answer later in the week. Write this Board as soon as possible. We are all well. Daddy is painting at Rosman.

lots of love,   Mama

*the mailman

Mr. Charles Allen McCall
RFD 1
Lake Toxaway, North Carolina

Dear Mr. McCall:

On July 12th, 1941, A form letter was
received from the U. S. Navy Recruiting Sub-Station,
Asheville, N. C., stating that you had been tentatively
accepted for enlistment in the U. S. Navy Reserve.
On July 27th, you wrote the Clerk of this Board, that
your address had been changed to Grover, N. C., and so
far as you knew you were going to the Navy September 1st,
but would keep us informed.
On August 18th a Form letter was mailed from U. S. Navy
Recruiting Station, Charlotte, N. C., stating that you
had enlisted in the U. S. Navy on that date.
Last week's Brevard paper, under personal items from
Rosman, there is the information that you have gone to
accept a position in defense work.
Please notify this Board at once your whereabouts and
occupation. This is very important.

Yours very truly
Transylvania County Local Board No. 1

By: *Alice B. Hardin*
Mrs. A. B. H Hill, Clerk.

Charles if I had time I write a letter
out Mr. Thomas is waiting one me I
got your letter just now will answer
later in the week. write this Board as
soon as possible. we are all well
daddy is painting at Rosman
lots of love Mama

326—43rd Street
Newport News, Va.
November 10, 1941

Dear Mama,

Your card and the paper came today. Glad to hear from you and also glad to know you are all getting along. O.K.

I am doing very well. I have been changed to day work and I like it somewhat better except for getting up so early. I made good on my first two weeks in welding school and was accepted for the experts course which will take be about three weeks longer. I wish I didn't have to go to the navy now, I could make some real money here for the next three or four years. After two months I would be making $125 per week which is not bad. Also, if I had come here before the draft got me I would have been exempt. That is all settled now, however, and there is nothing to be done about it.

I like this place O.K. I suppose. It is a regular boom town now with more money than I have ever seen There is 25,000 working in the shipyard where I am and lots of other big businesses. It is not my idea of a good place to live but it will do for a while.

They are really building ships up here. You will probably read about the launching of the battleship Indiana on the 21st of this month. I am working now right at the end of it and it is really some ship. It is 100% steel, not an ounce of wood on it and every piece of steel is welded on it so you can see how important welders are here. I would like for Jerry to be here and see some of the ships, he talks about them so much. I saw the British battleship "Queen of Burmuda" come in fresh from a battle and all shot to pieces the other day and I thought of some of those that Jerry used to make. I have talked a lot with the British sailors (an officer visited George and I in our room Saturday night) and believe me war is (with all sincerity and reverence) **hell**. *

The British officer that visited us was from Liverpool, England and while he was here we turned on the radio and heard that Hitler's bombs were over Liverpool and he sat there and told us about his wife and two babies there and cried like a baby. He hasn't seen or heard from them since 1939.

I spend all my spare time looking around and talking and finding out things like this so I could write you a book about it but I don't have time so I had just as well stop now.

I am rooming with George yet and will be right on I suppose. The place feels good and we like it fine. We go to church every Sunday at the First Baptist Church and it is really nice.

Write me soon.

Love,
Charles

P.S. I want you to send my overcoat, my best citizenship plaque, all *my* girls pictures (there are none here and I need some consolation), and any other odds and ends you think I might need. I want this insured, however, so wait until later in the week and I will send money for doing it.

C

* Someone had scratched out "hell" and I imagine that it was Grandma Delphie being true to her Southern Baptist roots!

Box 61
Brevard, N.C.
November 10, 1941

Dear Charles,

I guess you think I didn't appreciate your letter from the time I have taken answering it. I was glad to hear from you and know that you are doing alright.

Well I didn't get the chance to stick my neck out. I got notice yesterday from Washington that my application had been rejected. To young and not enough experience. I wish I could have got to the interview. I believe I could have sold them on my work. I certainly have worked on it. I think I'll hold steady for awhile and if I don't get caught in the army I'll make another try next summer at something else.

Charles I certainly do appreciate you giving me the tips on that job. Just hope I can repay you sometime.

Things have been right lively here since you left. *Five* girls have moved in just across the hall from me. How about coming down and helping cool them off? I let them get ahead of me, for I'm just not going to start taking them up town.

Are you keeping up with Duke's football score now? I heard the Duke-Davidson game over the radio the other day. 56-0 for Duke. That was to close, Duke will get beat if they don't do better than that.

I saw Ruth the other day. She had heard about us coming to her house and was very sorry that she was not home. She said for me to find out your address and she would mail your ring and pin to you. Do you want me to tell her your address or had you rather I would get the ring and pin and mail them myself? Let me know what you want me to do about it, if anything.

The deer hunt has started in the Forest this morning. I saw 20 or more up there the other night.

It is almost time to go to work so I guess I had better close and eat some.

Write when you can and I'll try to be here Christmas. (At least part of the time.

Your friend,
Leo Reid

P.S. If you can't read this blame these dam girls. They have pestered me all the time.

326—43rd Street
Newport News, Va.
November 23, 1941

Dear Mama,

Your letter and the package came O.K. Thanks a lot. The letter was real nice and I enjoyed it.

I am getting along fine now. I have gained 18 pounds since I have been here. I now weigh 174. It must have been the sea air or something. I am still in welding school, should be out in two or three days more.

Tell Ducky that I got her letter just three days ago. She addressed it wrong and just through luck I found it in the post office window. She put 236-43rd street instead of 326-43rd street and there is not a 236 on our street. Anyway I got it and will answer right away.

How is Helen and the baby getting along? I have planned to write them but haven't gotten around to it.

I want you to get together these three books: *Berlin Diary*—William L. Shirer, *Keys of the Kingdom*—A.G. Cronin, and *Diseases of Women* (a medicine book with black flexible backs) and mail them to Mrs. Frank Hambright, Grover, N.C. Thank you.

Write me soon for it sure is nice to hear from you. I enjoy the paper a lot.

Much love,
Charles A.

How is Helen and the baby getting along? I have planned to write them but haven't gotten around to it.

I want you to get together these three books: Berlin Diary - William L. Shirer, Keys of the Kingdom - A. J. Cronin, and Diseases of Women (a medicine book with black flexible backs) and mail them to Mrs. Frank Hambright, Grover, N.C. Thank you.

Write me soon for it sure is nice to hear from you. I enjoy the paper a lot.

Much love,
Charles A.

WESTERN UNION TELEGRAM
Newport News Vir 157pm 12/8/41*

Mirs Clyde S? Mccall

Lake Toxaway, N.E.

Leaving for home today hold all mail

Charles A Mccall

216pm

*The day after Pearl Harbor

WESTERN UNION

CLASS OF SERVICE

This is a full-rate Telegram or Cablegram unless its deferred character is indicated by a suitable symbol above or preceding the address.

1204

R. B. WHITE
PRESIDENT

NEWCOMB CARLTON
CHAIRMAN OF THE BOARD

J. C. WILLEVER
FIRST VICE-PRESIDENT

SYMBOLS

DL = Day Letter
NT = Overnight Telegram
LC = Deferred Cable
NLT = Cable Night Letter
Ship Radiogram

The filing time shown in the date line on telegrams and day letters is STANDARD TIME at point of origin. Time of receipt is STANDARD TIME at point of destination

    6 ge 7 Newport News Vir 157pm 12/8 /41
    Mirs Clyde S? Mccall

Lake Toxaway N.C.

Leaving for home today hold all mail

            Charles A Mccall

            216pm

WESTERN UNION
TELEGRAM

FOR QUICK SERVICE ANSWER BY BEARER

            Mrs Clyde S. Mccall

            Lake Toxaway N.C.

NUMBER 6	
CHARGES pd	Pay no charges on this message unless indicated on delivery sheet

★ ☆☆☆☆☆☆☆☆☆☆☆☆☆☆☆☆☆☆☆☆☆☆☆☆☆☆☆☆☆☆☆ ★

A Message from the
Commander-in-Chief of the Army and Navy of the United States
—*Franklin Delano Roosevelt*

From the White House, Washington, D. C., at 2200, Zone Plus Five Time, December 9, 1941.

THE sudden criminal attacks perpetrated by the Japanese in the Pacific provide the climax of a decade of international immorality. Powerful and resourceful gangsters have banded

In 1931, Japan invaded Manchoukuo—without warning.

In 1935, Italy invaded Ethiopia—without warning.

.F YEARS

page 9)

s celebrated

throughout
month of
ecially dear
: know when
There was
ind the Sec-
ieir cruise.
divided into
qual portions
i cruise; one
the summer.
arely Chesa-
it had an ad-
lass : most of
nand of a YP
t pleased the
y to be called
their absen-
down as they

just an inter-
mic routine.
usual. The

PRESIDENT ROOSEVELT'S SPEECH

(Continued from page 26)

On the other side of the picture, we must learn to know that guerrilla warfare against the Germans in Serbia helps us; that a successful Russian offensive against the Germans helps us; and that British successes on land or sea in any part of the world strengthens our hands.

Remember always that Germany and Italy, regardless of any formal declaration of war, consider themselves at war with the United States at this moment just as much as they consider themselves at war with Britain and Russia. And Germany puts all the other republics of the Americas into the category of enemies. The people of the hemisphere can be honored by that.

Destruction Not Aim

The true goal we seek is far above and beyond the ugly field of battle. When we resort to force, as now we must, we are determined that this force shall be directed toward ultimate good as well as against immediate evil. We Americans are not destroyers—we are builders.

We are now in the midst of a war, not for conquest, not for vengeance, but for a world in which this nation, and all that this nation represents, will be safe for our children. We expect to eliminate the danger from Japan, but it would serve us ill if we accomplished that and found that the rest of the world was dominated by Hitler and Mussolini.

We are going to win the war and we are going to win the peace that follows.

And in the dark hours of this day—and through dark days that may be yet to come—we will know that the vast majority of the members of the human race are on our side.

Many of them are fighting with us. All of them are praying for us. For in representing our cause, we represent theirs as well—our hope and their hope for liberty under God.

326—43rd St.
N. News, Va.
Thursday night
(December 1941)

Dear Charles:

Yesterday I got your money from the shipyard. This will come in very handy I am sure. To the tune of $19.70. Your papers from the Navy was sent just as soon as I came back. Mrs. Blodgett sent them. Did you get them?

Will try to get your clothes to you someway, as I am being drafted the 14th of Jan., but in the meantime I am trying to get set for the Navy reserve. I will work till then, C.

Had a swell Xmas, and got many presents. My nurse friend gave me a wrist watch worth around $40, sure was nice. Did you get my Xmas card?

Charles is this asking to much of you? If so just tell me. Due to this war situation no one will know just what can happen to us, so I am trying to leave everything in good shape just in case. My idea is to leave all my money and debts to my mama. When you get ready to pay it, you may send it to my mother. She is to use it for anything she may wish, but if not it is to be used to send my brs. to school this next year. So just send it to her.

Regardless of what has happened we will do our best won't we? So write me, and wish you much success and the very best of luck.

Your ole lady,
Geo.

Write me soon!

NEWPORT NEWS SHIPBUILDING AND DRY DOCK COMPANY

Newport News, Virginia   Dec. 23, 1941

As requested there is inclosed herewith our check payable to your order covering wages in full due you, as indicated.

NO ACKNOWLEDGMENT DESIRED

W. Graham Scott, Treasurer

Mr. C. A. McCall
326-43rd Street
Newport News, Virginia

yard check number	check number	amount
25202	418	$19.70

(Mr. Charles McCall
Lake Toxaway
North Carolina)

Shelby, N.C.
Dec. 28, 1941

Dear Charlie:

Was Santa good to you or had you been a bad boy? I've really had a merry, merry Christmas. The only bane is that it doesn't last long enough. I've looked for you to come every weekend since I got your letter. Please come to see us any time you can. We'll be back at Grover tomorrow. Do try hard to come. Mrs. Hamrick went to Washington for the holidays.

Jocelyn and I have your room now. The man teacher stayed in our room but I think he is going to stay at sister Lula's, if he returns. Mott still hangs around. Pinnix still gets her letter every day and Mary still calls us at fifteen minutes 'til seven. You better come see the changes that have been made—none in our looks except we have gained a few pounds. If something happens you don't get to come to see us keep writing to me. You're getting in a dangerous position. Be careful. That's the one thing I hate most about the draft. It takes the best—both physically and mentally.

John is still in Baltimore but doubts if he'll escape the draft. I haven't been up yet but I still want to go—to see him not to be drafted.

Our basketball teams aren't so good. Grade requirements took some of our best players out. Will tell rest when I see you.

Love,

Louise B.

On Friday, December 5, 1941, Grandpa Charlie attended the "SOS BLOWOUT" dinner/dance held at the Chamberlin Country Club, Newport News, and given for the Naval and Civilian Personnel of The Supervisor of Shipbuilding Office, USN. On Monday, he left for home to rest and spend the Christmas season with his family and friends. I know Grandma Delphie was happy to have her "boy" back in the nest; but it must have been a bitter-sweet holiday filled with both celebration and anxiety. I imagine the family spent considerable time gathered around the radio, discussing the attack on Pearl Harbor and the United States entry into World War II.

After Christmas, Grandpa Charlie prepared to attend The United States Naval Academy. His orders were to report to Annapolis January 9, 1942, with numerous items from the list they provided him in tow. His country was now at war and he was as about to pass through a door that would lead him far and farther still from Quebec, North Carolina.

CHAPTER FOUR

Midshipman at Annapolis

After the fall of France to the Axis powers in 1940, the United States, while maintaining a position of neutrality, began a significant and sustained increase in Navy personnel and ships. Subsequently, there became a great need for young Naval Officers to command newly commissioned ships and crews. The United States Naval Academy at Annapolis, Maryland instituted a compressed course of study to educate and train carefully chosen young men to meet this need.

Twenty-two year old Charles Allen McCall reported to the Naval Academy on January 9, 1942, at 8:00 a.m. He was embarking on an extremely intensive and competitive four month program. If successful, Grandpa Charlie would receive his commission as a U. S. Naval officer. He faced a rigorous challenge, described in the letters that follow.

(WNC Student Senate Stationery)

United States Naval Academy
Annapolis, Maryland
January 10, 1941(2)

Dear Mama,

My trip was O.K. and I arrived in good shape but a little tired. I got here about six o'clock yesterday morning and reported at eight. The remainder of the day was spent taking physical examinations and getting uniforms. I was given two vaccinations and a blood test all in one arm and it is rather sore. Today we have been more or less learning what it is all about. The military part of it begun as soon as we arrived, that is we were marched everywhere we went, required to salute officers, etc. The most difficult thing I have encountered yet is learning to fix the room properly. We have to fold every piece of clothing in a certain way, bed clothing must be folded exactly right, no dust must be left *anywhere*. I think I am going to like it a lot when I become more accustomed to things.

I only have about ten minutes for this letter so that leaves me only about time to say that I am exactly broke and need about five dollars as quickly as I can get it. I will repay it in two months. When you are writing me add my room number to the address I gave you (4230 Bancroft Hall)

Let me hear from you soon

Love, Charles

P.S. I am allowed to see no papers except those given us here so there is no need to send the county paper.

(WNC Student Senate Stationery)

Annapolis Maryland
January 18, 1941(2)

Dear Mama,

I received your letter with the money yesterday. Was mighty glad to hear from you, and the money sure did come in handy. You know the papers I received before I left home stated that I would only need ten dollars and we have already had to spend a little over twelve for shirts, gloves, and things like that.

I seem to be getting along O.K. here so far, however, the competition is pretty strong. Lots of the fellows here have had previous military experience and others have masters and doctors degrees. Sometimes I am afraid that I won't make the grade but am working awfully hard trying to. Twenty two men have already been sent home because of their failure to pass the physical requirements. We have had some pretty stiff physical exams such as swimming without touching bottom for thirty minutes, climbing up forty feet of vertical rope with our hands, swimming 50 feet under water, jumping, etc. Several were sent home at the beginning because of poor posture and failure in aptitude tests.

We all had a typhoid shot yesterday morning at nine thirty and it was so large by two o'clock over half the men had passed out cold. At dinner time it kept several men busy with stretchers carrying them out as they fell over. It didn't bother me quite so much, however. I have pretty well but am so sore I can hardly move. Things will be much better though if I last through the first month.

This is a wonderful place here, rich in history and tradition. The Museum has lots of old things which are very interesting.

Wendell Wilkie's son lives next door to me and I have become well acquainted with him. He is just one of the boys here, however, and so are all the other big shots sons who are here.

I have found out that I will have only one week-end (from Sat. noon until 5 Sunday) liberty before I finish so there will be no chance for me to get home. So far as I know I will have ten days after I finish.

Tell Jerry I enjoyed his card and to write me again. Let me hear from you soon.

Love,
Charles

U.S. Naval Academy
Annapolis, Maryland
Feb. 3, 1942

Dear Mama,

I have waited longer than I should have to write you but I wrote just a day or two before I heard from you last so I was waiting to hear from you.

I am getting along fine right at present with the exception of a little injury. I got a rib fractured the other day wrestling and am all braced up but it doesn't bother me very much. I am still going ahead with my drill and class work so it doesn't keep me behind in the more important things.

Our elimination period will be over at the end of this week at which time approximately 25% of us will be kicked out. If I last through that I will stand a much better chance of lasting through the course. After that, however, most of our work will be in the classroom and will be plenty hard. We have already been issued text books and, judging from their looks, I am going to have to really put out to make it.

Naval officers are supposed to be practically perfect in every respect and, believe me, this institution believes in making them that way. This training will sure be valuable to a person later on if he can acquire and use all the good habits that they are forcing us to learn.

I don't think I will need a sweater now since most of the outside drill is over. I could have used it to a great advantage before this but have made out O.K. without it.

I am rather tired and can't think of very much to write just now. The war situation from here looks pretty dark right at present. I don't think there is any doubt at all as to its outcome but it is going to be long, costly, and exciting. The moral of this group is exceedingly good, in fact, we can hardly wait to get into it and see some of the fireworks but we realize the foolishness of "sticking your neck out" so we are contented to get in position and lay low waiting for the thrilling moment when the knock out blow can be landed. There is more going on than you on the outside know about but which I cannot talk about. We are loosing no tricks that have not been anticipated.

Give everyone my regards and write me soon.

Much love,
Charles

United States Naval Academy
Annapolis, Maryland
Feb. 12, 1941(42)

Dear Mama,

Our classwork has begun and it seems that I can never find time to write. After being rushed from 6 A.M. to 6:30 P.M. I hardly feel like writing during the thirty minutes from then until supper, and after supper I have to pull my hair until lights out in order to get by the next day. Since my assignment for tomorrow is a little lighter I am taking this opportunity to write.

I am in a position where it is hard to say whether I am O.K. or in a mess. This electrical engineering and hydrodynamics is just about over my head—that is—at the rate we are expected to learn it. Some of these guys are already experts at that sort of thing and we poor fellows who are not just have to hang on and keep up if we can. We are supposed to absorp a four year course in three months and believe me it is *plenty tough*.

I am going to have two days off on Feb. 21 & 22. If I could get enough money to go over to Washington to spend the night it would be wonderful to get away from here for the change just that long. If you can locate a little some place I sure would appreciate it. If not, I will make the best of it here.

Write to me and tell me the news.

Much love,
Charles

United States Naval Academy
Annapolis, Maryland
February 13, 1941(2)

Dear Mama,

The cigarettes came today and, boy!, I sure was glad to get them. It sure was sweet of you to send them and I really appreciate it. Mama, I don't want you and Daddy to feel responsible for sending me money and things like that because I am much beyond that age. I know I shouldn't ask for it and if you don't have it don't hesitate or feel badly about telling me so. I suppose I am still a little childish—and you folks are responsible for it for treating me so good.

I am getting along O.K. now. I feel good, have lots to eat, get plenty of exercise, and enough sleep. I am weighing around 175, the most I ever have. So don't get the idea that I am being treated badly or overworked, it's just that I have never been kept so busy. I use about 16 hours of every day at some advantageous task, while up to now I have never used more than 10. A person never realizes how much time he is really wasting until he is required to use it all. For instance, I never sit around and rest after meals or between jobs. From six in the morning until 11 at night the only time I have to do as I please is from 6:30 to 7 p.m. We can always do much more than we think is humanly possible if we have to, and it's good for us if we are not lazy.

Well, its supper time and I'll have to close. Give everyone my regards and write soon.

Much love,
Charles

(on WNC Student Senate Stationery)

United States Naval Academy
Annapolis, Maryland
February 18, 1942

Dear Daddy,

Your letter and the five bucks came today. I sure do thank you for it—more than I can say. I just hope you didn't have to sacrifice too much to send it because I wouldn't want it under those circumstances.

You asked when I was going to get paid—and that I just learned today. At the end of this month, and the next two months, I will be paid the grand sum of $12. Of course, I am making $75 per month but all but 12 is being held for my uniforms. I'll have enough for my needs, of course, from here on out but I'm afraid I will be unable to help you for a few months. As soon as I am in the position I'll help you every way possible. $500 worth of uniforms are going to be hard to pay for.

I thought I had acknowledged the $ and cigarettes. The letter must have been lost. Anyway, they came and I sure appreciate them.

I am standing 24 hour watch today and right now is the only 30 min. rest I have so I'll close and try to lay down and rest. It's rather tiresome to walk constantly for eight hours and at the same time carry an 8 lb. rifle and a sword and a .45 automatic pistol.

Write soon,
Charles

United States Naval Academy
Annapolis, Maryland
February 18, 1942

Dear Daddy,

Your letter and the five bucks came today. I sure do thank you for it — more than I can say. I just hope you didn't have to sacrifice too much to send it because I wouldn't want it under those circumstances.

You asked when I was going to get paid — and that I just learned today. At the end of this month, and the next two months, I will be paid the grand sum of $12. Of course, I am making $75 per month but all but 12 is being held for my uniforms. I'll have enough for my needs, of course, from here on out but I'm afraid I will be unable to help you for a few months. As soon as I am in the position I'll help you every way possible. $800 worth of uniforms are going to be hard to pay for.

I thought I had acknowledged the $ and cigarettes. The letter must have been lost. anyway, they came and I sure appreciate them.

I am standing 24 hour watch today and right now is the only 30 min. rest I have so I'll close and try to lay down and rest. It's rather tiresome to walk constantly for eight hours and at the same time carry an 8 lb. automatic rifle and a sword, and a .45 automatic pistol.

Write soon.
Charles

ANNAPOLIS
FEB 19
6 AM
1942
MD.

NAVAL ACADEMY

BRANCH

3 CENTS

Mr. Clyde S. McCall

Lake Junaluska

NAVAL ACADEMY BRANCH

ANNAPOLIS
FEB 19
6 AM
1942

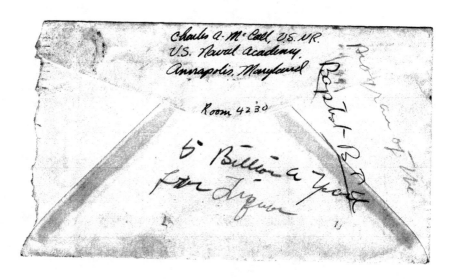

Charles A. McCall, U.S. N.R.
U.S. Naval Academy.
Annapolis, Maryland.

Room 4230

6 Billion a Year
for Liquor

United States Naval Academy
Annapolis, Maryland
March 1, 1942

Dear Mama

I'm soory I haven't written sooner this week but since I was away last week-end I had to work harder and didn't find time. Thanks for your letter and the dollar. I sure did use the dollar to a great advantage but you needn't send any more. I will get a pay day (of$12) within the next few days and can get along fine on that.

Yes, I went to Washington last week-end and had a wonderful time. I left here Saturday afternoon and got there in about an hour. I spent the rest of the afternoon looking around at the sights. Sunday morning I went to the church where the president usually goes but he was not there. I spent Sunday afternoon in the Smithsonian Institute which was extremely interesting. I saw Lindberg's plane, a lot of Edison's original work, famous papers, properties of Washington and the other presidents, and a million other things. While I was there I ran into a girl from Cullowhee (working there) and she invited me out to supper. After supper we went to the library of congress to see the famous papers and paintings and read a while. Monday morning I went to the Senate Chamber and listened to them (and later the House) until one o'clock. I saw and heard Wallace, Glass, Tydings, and most of the other big shots (Bob Reynolds too—Bailey was not there). I went to Reynold's office to see him but he was out at that time. The Capitol building was very interesting as well as the White house and other Government buildings. Monday was Washington's birthday, you know, and I went over to the Washington monument to the program they had. Of all the things I saw, I was impressed more by the Lincoln memorial than any other thing. I saw the president for a moment as he was leaving the White House but it was so closely guarded I couldn't get very close.

Washington is a beautiful city but is so crowded now it is hard to get around. It is full of guards and soldiers. On top of every building you can see three or four anti-aircraft guns manned and ready for action. I had a nice room in a tourist home for $1.50 per night which was very lucky considering the crowded conditions.

The week-end away from here did me a lot of good and proved very restful. I am getting along fine now, still working awfully hard and wondering if I will last through. At the end of every week a list of all those who have unsatisfactory grades is posted on the bulletin board. I haven't been on the list yet but can't be missing it much I am afraid. This is the first time I have ever had any trouble staying at or near the head of the class and I find it right discouraging. I think I could still do it if we were all studying something new, but in this case I am supposed to know a lot of things I have never studied before this and that makes it extremely difficult.

I have been seeing a lot of famous people around here lately. The crown prince and princess of Norway were at church (or chapel as we call it) this morning along with their Field Marshall—a very interesting group.

I can get the county paper now if you will send it. For a while we were only allowed to read certain Newspapers but for some reason that restriction has been removed.

Yes, the war situation gets worse all the time. Of course it is not hard to understand why when all the factors are considered. I thought the president's speech was pretty good from the geographical point of view. If every one could understand all the problems connected with assembling, transporting, and putting into action *properly* of troops and supplies there would be much less growling and fussing. I know we could send 500,000 men to the far East and find some fighting for them to do very easily but there are a million factors to consider. What makes me so mad and what is causing more dissatisfaction among the armed forces than any other thing is these industrial strikes and disorder. On the front page of the "Washington Post" the other day there were two columns side by side; one entitled "Phillip Murray's Boys refuse to work long hours without highly increased pay", the other entitled "McArthur's Boys pool money to buy planes." That expresses the feeling. If a group of soldiers can save money to buy bombers on their $21 a month then why can't the boys back home work a few more hours a week for a hundred. I have always been able to sympathize with labor unions but I can't see their point now.

Well, it's supper time and I'll have to close. Write me soon. Ask Helen, when you see her, if she got the letter I wrote her. I wasn't sure of the address.

> Much love,
> Charles

UNITED STATES NAVAL ACADEMY
ANNAPOLIS, MARYLAND

March 13, 1941(42)

Dear Mama,

Was glad to hear from you and tell Jerry that his card was just as good as a college professor could do and I enjoyed it more. Ducky's letter came too and she is to be highly complimented for all the reading she has done. I'm sorry I haven't gotten around to answering all of them yet, but I will as soon as I can find time.

Is the snow all gone? I sure hate that I had to miss it. We didn't have any at all here, in fact, it has been regular Spring weather here for the past three weeks.

I haven't heard from John at all since I have been here. I suppose he and Helen just don't care for writing and Helen is very busy now I guess.

I am getting along very well now so far as I can tell. The work is not any easier, if there is any change at all it gets harder all the time. Next week will end the first term and we will have two-day examinations. There will probably be about 100 boys kicked out when that is over. I am keeping my fingers crossed.

I'll have to close as the time is short. Write soon.

Much love,
Charles

UNITED STATES NAVAL ACADEMY
ANNAPOLIS, MARYLAND

Saturday
March 17, 1942

Dear Mama,

I finished my examinations today at twelve o'clock and don't have anything to do the rest of the day and it sure is wonderful. It's raining here and I'm awfully sleepy so you can guess how I will spend the afternoon.

I'm afraid to say how I did on the examinations. They were plenty tough. I feel pretty sure that I passed but you never can tell at this place. One fellow was turned out last week because he failed electrical engineering and before he came here he was an electrical research engineer for Westinghouse. Some of the instructors don't know very much and if your answers aren't direct quotations from the textbook they count them wrong.

I went out last week and was measured up for four hundred dollars worth of uniforms. It's hard to see how you can put that much money in as little an amount of things that I got. The Navy tells you what to buy and how much to buy, however, so there was nothing I could do about it. Of course, everything I got had to be of the best quality made but that was probably good since I will more than likely be wearing it for the next two years. I got two blue dress uniforms at $60 each, four white dress uniforms at $15 each, Two tan work uniforms at $15 each, two caps at $15 each, one raincoat at (imagine this) $59, One formal outfit (scissor-tails & tuxedo) for $60, and a sword for $40. Some of the things seem useless but I'm required to have them. I'll have to pay $90 for an overcoat sometime before winter as well as a bunch of shirts, shoes, etc. Sometimes I wish I were in the Army.

I enjoyed the cards from "General" and private. Give everyone my regards.

Much love,
Charles

UNITED STATES NAVAL ACADEMY
ANNAPOLIS, MARYLAND

3/27/42

Dear Mama,

Was glad to hear from you and know that everyone is getting along O.K. I suppose you enjoyed Grandma's visit. It is good to know that she is still able to get around as well.

From the question you asked as to what I meant by boys failing out here I see that you don't understand the nature of what I am in. In effect, this is just a highly condensed college engineering course. We go to classes, have laboratory work, text books (loads of them) and everything just like college. The only difference is that here, instead of having examinations weekly or monthly, we have them daily. We are assigned around fifty or one hundred pages for each class and one hour recitation. The first thirty minutes of the recitation period we may ask questions concerning the lesson and the last thirty we have a test. The daily grades are averaged for a weekly grade and these are averaged with final examination grade for the term grade. All grades below 80% are failures and all failures are posted weekly. A failing grade in two subjects for one week or a failing grade in one subject two weeks automatically fails you out. About seventy five boys were sent home after finals last week leaving only about ½ of the original number here that we had when we begun.

In addition to curricular grades we are graded on "aptitude" which includes personal appearance, dress, cleanliness, physical ability, leadership, etc. This grade counts just as much as the others.

You probably have the idea that this is something like the army but that is *entirely* wrong. The army reaches out and gets you but Navy officers are lucky to get in and have to work plenty hard to stay in. As important as quantity is right now, the quality of Naval officers has not been lowered even slightly. A naval officer is intelligent, knows his machinery and ship thoroughly, is a gentleman, a leader—and if he isn't all this and more the Navy has no use for him and doesn't fail to tell him so. People use the expression "He curses like a sailor" which may be partially true of enlisted men but an officer would never think of it. In fact a boy here gets ten demerits for even using a shady expression.

So you see this is not a case of being drafted—it is a case of working plenty hard to stay in.

How is Daddy's work? I hope he is getting along fine with it. Has he bought his tires?

Glad to hear that Roy likes his work and that he and Helen are getting along O.K. I'm anxious to see the baby. And too, I am expecting Joe Ben to be able to carry on a conversation with me when I get home.

The paper came and I found it very interesting. Where is M.O. and J.B. now?

So far as I know now I will be home about May 7th. All I want is you to have me a fish hook, frying pan, and a blanket ready.

Write soon.

Love,
Charles

UNITED STATES NAVAL ACADEMY
ANNAPOLIS, MARYLAND

4/2/42

Dear Mama,

I have just about ten minutes before lights out so I write just a note.

Your letter came today. Thanks for the pictures, they are good and I enjoyed them. Helen wrote and sent me a picture of her and Suzzane.

I am getting along fine now so far as I know. We had a 19 inch snow here Sunday but it is all gone now and Spring weather is here again. Had Saturday night off and went up to Baltimore—had a nice time.

I took out a $10,000 life insurance policy last week and named you as beneficiary. You will receive the policy to hold sometime within the next two months. It is a Gov. policy and is O.K. but you should check over it carefully and be sure you understand the terms—consult a lawyer if necessary.

Write soon—Good night

Charles

UNITED STATES NAVAL ACADEMY
ANNAPOLIS, MARYLAND
4/2/42

Dear Mama,

I have just about two minutes before lights out so I write just a note.

Your letter came today. Thanks for the picture, they are good and I enjoyed them. Helen wrote and sent me a picture of her and Suzzon.

I am getting along fine now so far as I know. We had a 19 inch snow here Sunday but it is all gone now and Spring weather is here again. Had Saturday night off and went up to Baltimore — had a nice time.

I took out a $10,000 life insurance policy last week and named you as beneficiary. You will receive the policy to hold sometime within the next two months. It is a Gov. policy and is O.K. but you should check over it carefully and be sure you understand the terms — consult a lawyer if necessary.

Write soon — Good night

Charles.

UNITED STATES NAVAL ACADEMY
ANNAPOLIS, MARYLAND

4/10/42

Dear Mama,

Your letter came yesterday and has caused me no end of worry. I can sympathise with the way you feel since it is only natural for you to feel that way and I love you for it, however, I would be much happier if you didn't. I can easily see your viewpoint, and as for doing something for me, I don't see how any boy could ever hope for his parents to do more for him than you have done for me. You have sacrificed more than you really should have and my deepest regret is that I am unable to repay you in the way you deserve pay. I would enjoy being with you just as much as you would enjoy having me but the world isn't run that way.

If you really want to do something for me, which I know you do, try to understand how I feel about the situation. *Under the present circumstances* there is no place in all the world I had rather be than where I am right now. I am in good physical and moral surroundings, I have a definite goal which I am having to work awfully hard to attain and this will do any man lots of good, my position places me in the upper five percent in intelligence, physical qualities, moral qualities, education, and culture of all people in United States, and will shortly place me in the upper twenty five percent financially; I am healthy, happy and your son—what more could I ask for?

How do you think I would feel, and how would you feel if I (a strong able bodied man) were sitting at home on my tail while the country we love and the country which makes and gives homes and parents like I have was being insulted and threatened of annihilation. I am just not made up right to stand by and see things like that go on—so I'll choose my lot here and make the most of it. Please try to see it this way, Mama, and don't worry about me. After all, isn't your greatest wish for me to see me happy? Well, that wish is granted—and I mean it from the depths of my heart. Someday soon it will all be over and all you will have to worry about will be whether or not I am spoiling your grandson too much. Lets look forward to that day and consider these next few as a light case of measles which will keep us in bed a little while—what do you say?

Yes, I will be home in a little less than four weeks now. I am looking forward to seeing you all and a nice quiet rest.

I am enclosing a few snaps which were taken here and there, hope you enjoy them.

Write soon and give everyone my regards.

Love,
Chas.

P.S. I save the quotation in the paper taken from my letter which was quite allright but please remember that my letter are personal so please see that they don't get any further than the immediate family at the most. If the paper wants an article they should consult me for direct quotations and if any of our friends want a letter, let them write me first.

UNITED STATES NAVAL ACADEMY
ANNAPOLIS, MARYLAND

4/21/'42

Dear Mama,

The box came Sunday and your letter today. The cookies were real good and I certainly did enjoy them, thank you lots. The cigarettes also came in handy.

Well, I started to write you Tuesday and just got this far and here it is Friday and I'm just getting around to finishing. It is so hard to find time to write that my letters are few and far between.

There is just a little more than a week to go now and I must say I'm not sorry. I will be glad to get my head out of a text book and most of all I will be glad to get home again even if it is for just a short time.

I got my orders the other day telling me where I am going after this and when. I can't even give you a hint as to their contents, however, even though I know you are anxious to know. The statement I made concerning your quoting my letters sounded very harsh and I didn't mean to offend you or daddy, perhaps you will understand if I give you a little incident. A fellow who graduated here a few months ago wrote home and told his family where he was going and the ship he was assigned to. Somehow or other it got into a small town paper and as soon as the fellow reported he was court martialed and given a dishonorable discharge. As a result of that we have been given orders to disclose *no* information of any kind to *any* one. Even small personal incidents which would seemingly be absolutely harmless are to go no further than our immediate families. So you see I (and you) must be very careful. I can tell you a few things when I get home but don't expect too much. We have been instructed to answer all questions with the words, "I don't know where I have been, I don't know where I am going and I can't tell you which ship I am on." So when anyone asks about me you might tell them I am getting along fine and then give them that quotation. Of course, there is no secret about where I am now, but you know how easily rumors get started and any of them could give me plenty of trouble. In this connection I might give you a hint as to why my letters are late sometimes—(can you think of a better place to study the operation of naval machinery than on a ship at sea?)

Saw the Asheville paper this week and noticed you have some serious forest fires. Have they been close home?

I'm plenty mad at that John for not having written me, I'll see him about it when I get home and you had better warn him—and you had better warn him because I'm 6 ft ½ in, weigh 183, an expert boxer, wrestler, and expert at ju-jitsu, rough-and tumble, plenty tough and hard as a rock. And also—in case he really wants to get Tough, I just finished third in our regiment with the .45 cal. Pistol with a score of 93/100 and am on the fencing (sword fighting) team.

Tell Jerry that I'm afraid I will be unable to bring my sword home with me this time since I will only get it the day before I leave and am going to leave it here to get it engraved and have it sent to me later. I will have the belt I wear it on, though, and will tell him all about it. And in turn I'm depending on him to have our fish-hooks and on Dan to tell us where we can find some red worms.

I am enclosing a clipping from the paper you might be interested in. I'm in the picture but so far away you couldn't recognize me.

Write soon

Love,
Charles

UNITED STATES NAVAL ACADEMY
ANNAPOLIS, MARYLAND

5/2/42

Dear Mama,

Classes are all over, I have had all the final exams and it sure is a wonderful feeling. Tomorrow we check in all of our books, linen, uniforms, etc. Graduation exercises are Tuesday morning at ten o'clock and I'll be ready to leave here either Tuesday night or Wednesday morning.

I am looking forward with a great deal of pleasure to the trip home for this reason—I am going to fly from Washington to Charleston. I have always wanted to do something like that and this is a good opportunity. I am allowed .8 per mile for traveling and I can fly easily on that.

We are having the regular commencement exercises—had the sermon today, farewell party tomorrow night, etc. I think Admiral Hart is going to present our commissions. He was here today and through pure good fortune I sat by him in chapel—some thrill. We are having an awfully hard time getting our uniforms. The taylor I contracted with had a shortage at the last moment and left me in a jam. I went to Washington yesterday, however, and finished out my outfit I think. I couldn't think of going home without some of these snappy whites to show off.

Tell Sue that her invitation came and I wanted to write her and express my congratulations but with finals and all I just haven't been able to.

I don't know about the bus schedules out of Asheville or Brevard but if Daddy finds it convenient he might come down to Brevard about six o'clock Wednesday afternoon and look for me if I am not already home.

Will see you soon

Much love
Charles

The Class of Reserve Midshipmen

of the

United States Naval Academy

announce their exercises for

commissioning as Ensigns

in the

United States Naval Reserve

Dahlgren Hall

Tuesday, May fifth

nineteen hundred forty-two

Free

Mr. and Mrs. Clyde S. McCall and Family
Lake Toxaway, North Carolina

CHAPTER FIVE

Charleston and Ohio State

Charles Allen McCall, Sr., graduated from the United States Naval Academy on May 5, 1942, and was commissioned an Ensign in the U.S. Navy. He left immediately thereafter for his North Carolina mountain homeplace. Grandpa Charlie was most excited about flying from Annapolis to Charleston, South Carolina. His previous journeys had been by train and bus, which he would have to employ again for the trip on home from Charleston. He had accomplished a mighty task and was quite proud of himself. I have had a copy of the professional photograph of Grandpa Charlie wearing his dress whites displayed in my home for many years, but only now do I know the story behind that picture. Isn't it funny how a familiar photograph can take on new life when its story is told. I'm not so sure anymore of the old saying "a picture is worth a thousand words." These letters are as valuable as our old photographs. How fortunate we are to have them both.

Grandpa Charlie spent a couple of weeks at home with his family and friends before traveling back to Charleston, South Carolina where he reported for Navy duty. The next of his letters are written from Charleston and Columbus, Ohio. The Navy sent him from Charleston to Ohio State University in Columbus for an intensive course in the "Engineering, Science, and Management War Training Program." The time at Ohio State proved to be most interesting for Grandpa Charlie, both academically and personally. So, read on, my precious ones.

UNITED STATES NAVAL ACADEMY
ANNAPOLIS, MARYLAND

(May 22, 1942)
62 Montague Street
Charleston, S.C.

Dear Mama,

I have time for just a word. I am out at sea on patrol duty everyday and here every night for an indefinite time. Three boys and I have an apartment here which is very nice but sky high (as is everything here) in price.

I am well pleased with my work and having a wonderful time but awfully busy. How is everyone there?

It is very hot here but I am right down at the sea and there is a nice breeze at night which makes it very comfortable.

I left a picture over at "Murtie's" Store I want some of you to send to me.

Write often and I will answer as often as possible.

Much love,
Charles

Confidential
U. S. S. EXULTANT (AMc 79)

Friday Night
(June 6, 1942)

Dear Mama,

I have been on a little trip and just got back today. Hope you haven't been too worried about not hearing from me. I am getting along fine and having a wonderful time. Will try to write at every opportunity but if there are times when you don't hear from me for several days please don't worry about it. I am living a very comfortable but very busy life with not too much to do but it keeps me busy staying ahead of my men and keeping them on their toes. I think I'll make a sailor yet.

How is every one there? I have gotten your letters for which I am very thankful. Please write as often as you can for I am always glad to hear from you. Give my regards to Helen and John and tell them to write. Also tell John that I would like to have the address you gave him.

It is very hot in Charleston now but very comfortable out at sea and I am spending most of my time at sea now so the heat doesn't bother me. You should see my sun tan, I'm the blackest I've ever been. The sun really bears down out there but you don't notice it being hot because of the breezes. We hit a very rough sea the other day and almost every one on the ship got sick but I didn't feel the least bit bad—a born seaman I suppose?

I had the cyst removed from my face just after I got down here and it is already well. It was a right painful little operation and required two stitches but it is all over now and I don't believe the scar will be noticeable at all.

Tell Daddy and all the kids hello for me, wish I could see them.

I enjoy the paper very much.

All my love
Charles

U. S. S. EXULTANT (AMc 79)

Friday Night

Dear Mama,

I have been on a little trip and just got back today. Hope you haven't been too worried about not hearing from me. I am getting along fine and having a wonderful time. Will try to write at every oppertunity but if there are times when you don't hear from me for several days please don't worry about it. I am living a very comfortable but very busy life with not too much to do but it keeps me busy staying ahead of my men and keeping them on their toes. I think I'll make a sailor yet.

How is every one there? I have gotten your letters for which I am very thankful. Please write as often as you can for I am always glad to hear from you. Give my regards to Helen and John and tell them to write. Also tell John that I would like to have the address you gave him.

It is very hot in Charleston now but very comfortable out at sea and I am spending most of my time at sea now so the heat doesn't bother me. You should see my sun tan, I'm the blackest I've ever been. The sun really bears down out there but you don't notice it being hot because of the breezes. We hit a very rough sea the other day and almost every one on the ship got sick but I didn't feel the least bit bad--a born seaman I suppose?

I had the cyst removed from my face just after I got down here and it is already weal. It was a right painful little operation and required two stitches but it is all over now and I don't believe the scar will be noticable at all.

Tell Daddy and all the kids hello for me, wish I could see them.

I enjoy the paper very much.

All my love

Charles

USS EXULTANT
c/o Postmaster, New York
(no date)

Dear Mama,

I wonder if you have worried about not hearing from me. I have been fine and am having a wonderful time. I miss you folks, of course, but outside of that I have never been happier. I enjoy my work and everything is perfect. As you will notice, I am permenantly assigned to a ship now and like that much better than living ashore.

How is everyone there? I had a letter from you yesterday and it sure was nice to hear from you. Write often even if I can't.

Has Roy gone away yet? How is Helen and the baby, John and his wife? Give them all my regards and tell them to write me.

Have you received my insurance policy yet? Let me know when it comes. I would also like to know if you hear anything from Cullowhee about my notes. I am going to pay all of them off at the end of this month. I have almost enough for that now but am waiting to pay it all at once.

There isn't much I can say except that I am well, happy and satisfied.

Love,
Charles

Ohio State
University   July 8, 1942

Dear Mama,

Had a very pleasant trip, am all settled down and hard at work. This is a very beautiful place and they have everything necessary for a wonderful college education.

I will be in school six days a week from eight until five thirty. The work will be plenty tough but very interesting and helpful. It is much cooler here than in Charleston and that sure is a great help.

Mallonee is here—it seems that we two are almost inseparable. That is very good, however, since I like him a lot and it is quite a help to have an old friend around.

Is the picture I have of Irene there? If it is please send it to me.

Give everyone my regards and write often.

                                                    Love,
                                                    Charles

Box 309 Baker Hall
Ohio State University
Columbus, Ohio
July 25, 1942

Dear Mama,

I have been a little slow about writing but have hardly felt like it
for the last few days. The wisdom tooth I had so much trouble with
last summer has been acting up exactly the same way and has been
just about running me into fits. It won't get any better or come to a
head so it can be lanced so I am going under gas tonight and have
it extracted. It will probably give me some trouble for a few days but
anything would be welcomed if I can only get rid of this.

The card came yesterday and the cigarettes today. It was sweet of
you to remember me and send them. Thanks a million. It so happens
that the cigarettes are very welcome right now. We don't have a pay
master here yet and have not been paid! With the expenses up here
and sixty dollars in advance for room & board for a month I am almost
broke. We will get our checks on the 30th, however, and a month's
salary plus traveling expenses up here I will be pretty well fixed.

I had a wonderful birthday, Mama. To tell you about it I will have
to begin with the second day I was here. It all boils down to this—I
met the most wonderful girl I have ever known. I was introduced
to her by one of the professors here and after a rather drawn out
conversation I asked if I might call on her that night. She gave me her
address and I proceeded to go out. I found the house but was soon
lost—so to speak—It was a very large and beautiful home and when
I rang the bell the door was opened by a butler who asked for my
hat & card. He led me through two or three drawing rooms, etc. and
I felt like "Alice in Wonderland." She came down & I met her family
and we all got along fine. I have seen her every night since then that
I could get away. She is very "down to earth", extremely intelligent
and agrees with me on practically everything. She's beautiful and
perhaps just a little high class for me but she's crazy about me and
after all why should I be so particular when she insists that I keep
one of her buicks all the time for my own personal use. Well, on my
birthday she invited me out to dinner at the country club. Mallonee

went along with me for her girl friend (he's doing O.K. too) and we had a five course dinner—steaks, birthday cake with my name on it, and everything. There was four of us and when the waiter brought the bill around for $26 I almost fainted. All she had to do however, was sign her dad's name to it and it was all fixed. Her dad has had me out to play golf with him several times and I'm standing in. He has a group of thirty offices in a skyscraper here with an office force of over a hundred. He is a personal friend of the president and I have already met the governor of Ohio through him. Well, that's enough about the gal, guess I sound rather childish but I do like her a lot. How do you think I would get along with a wife like that? Don't get excited, though, she has two more years of college yet.

John has never mentioned anything to me about the suit. I suppose I may as well give it to him. If he says anything more about it, give it to him if you think he needs it. It will probably be rotton or out of style before I need it anyway. Looks like he could write to me. It is quite possible that his big brother will be in a position to give him some real help some day.

I had a letter and a birthday card from Helen. She told me that Roy was in Baltimore and she expected to go soon. Hope she likes it—it sure is a nice place there. She also told me that Daddy was dressed out in a nice outfit the last time she saw him. Sure is nice and I know he was glad to get it.

School is rather stiff but nothing too hard. Most of it is the type that does not require much study at night and I think that is wonderful. The nights are cool and it sure is good sleeping. After living on three or four hours sleep each night for so long it sure is swell to be able to get six or eight. I haven't been to classes the last two days because of my tooth nor gotten much sleep for that matter.

How is Ducky & the boys. Give them all my regards. Seems that Sue could write sometime since she can't find any other boys to write to (did that make her mad?)

Write often & thanks again for remembering my birthday.

Love,
Charles

(Columbus, Ohio
July 18, 1942)

Dear Mama,

If the prof. don't catch me I will try to write just a few lines. I am in class and so sleepy I have to do something to keep my eyes open. It is rather hot here this morning and four hours lecture becomes rather monotonous after so long a time.

How is everyone there? I sure do miss that part of the country especially along about now when it is so hot. It is much cooler here than in Charleston but they still don't have those good cool nights like you do there. This is beautiful country, however, and I like it a lot. Wouldn't mind living here.

I want to go over to Atkins one Sunday before long to see the Galloways but I don't know exactly where to go so I wonder if you will help me. The next time you are at Toxaway or see some of their folks find out their address and send it to me.

I am being kept rather busy here but have much more time for rest and recreation than I had before I came. I am having a very good time along with the work. There are 7,000 in Summer School so I meet a lot of people, swim, play tennis, etc. when I have time.

From the word I have now I will only be here until the middle of September. I don't know where to after that but hope I have time to come by home a few days.

Wish you would send me Sue's address. I think I know Helen's. I wrote her a card the other day. Write often.

Love,
Charles

OHIO STATE

August 15, 1942

Dear Mama,

Hope you are all well. I am doing fine now that my jaw is well. The tooth is ready to be pulled and I plan to have that done sometime this week.

It will only be four weeks now until I am through here. I don't know whether I will be able to get home after that or not. I will probably not have any leave but if I report to any port South of here I probably will have time to come by. I haven't received any orders yet so don't have any idea where I will go.

Has Helen moved yet? How is she, Suzanne, and Roy? I had a letter from John a few days ago concerning the suit. I am writing him to take it.

Has the weather begun to get cool there yet? We are having some very cool nights.

I had some pictures made the other day and will send you one as soon as they are finished.

What is Daddy doing now? Sure would like to see you all.

Write often and tell me how everyone is. Try to forgive me if my letters are rather far apart, I'm very busy and awfully lazy.

Lots of love,
Charles

(Columbus, Ohio
Sept. 1, 1942)

Dear Mama,

Hope you have heard from me since you wrote last. I'm very sorry you worried so much because I hadn't written but I didn't realize I had waited so long.

Everything is fine here. It has been rather cold here for the last few days which they say is very unusual for this time of year but which is very pleasant. The mornings feel just like late fall, makes me want to go squirrel hunting.

There seems to be a little confusion here as to when our class will be through. I am pretty sure it will be either on the 12th or 26th of next month. Sure hope I will be able to get home a little while. I still have no further orders.

Is Helen gone now? If so will you send me her address. What kind of job does Roy have?

I haven't written or been out to see Galloways yet so I'm still not certain where they live. The two towns you listed are not so far apart and only about one hundred miles from here so I think Sally and I will drive out there maybe next Sunday and look them up.

I'm very anxious to find out how Jerry gets along in school. Is Dan going too? Guess you feel rather deserted when they all got gone, Don't you? Is Sue at home?

I'm sending Jerry and Dan a little package. I can't be sure about size but in case the things don't fit send them back right away and I'll exchange them. I'm a little afraid of how Ducky may feel but please explain to her that she will be next and it will not be so very long. I'm also enclosing a picture for you in the package.

Write soon.

Love,
Charles

OHIO STATE

September 7, 1942

Dear Mama,

Just have time for a few lines. I haven't heard from you in several days and am wondering how everyone is. I got Daddy's letter last week and enjoyed it very much. Too bad about Ducky's arm. Is it better now?

I still don't have any definite orders and don't know exactly where I'm going or how long I will have. I am planning to get home, however, and have a plane reservation for Saturday afternoon to Knoxville Tennesse and will take the first train or bus out of there which should put me home sometime Sunday or Monday. Will wire if there is any change.

Everything here is just about wound up except final examinations, packing and getting out. I've had a very enjoyable stay here which I think has proven very educational also and I hate to leave. There is a war to be fought, however, so I guess I'll have to move along.

Much love,
Chas.

September 7, 1942

Dear Mama,

Just have time for a few lines I haven't heard from you in several days and am wondering how everyone is. I got Daddy's letter last week and enjoyed it very much. Too bad about Ducky's arm. Is it better now?

I still don't have any definite orders and don't know exactly where I'm going or how long I will have. I am planning to get home, however, and have a plane reservation for Saturday afternoon to Knoxville Tennessee and will take the first train or bus out of there which should put me home sometime Sunday or Monday. Will wire if there is any change.

Everything here is just about wound up except final examinations, packing and getting out. I've had a very enjoyable stay here which I think has proven very educational also and I hate to leave. There is a war to be fought, however, so I guess I'll have to move along,

Much love,
Chas.

CHAPTER SIX

Amphibious Training and Hospitalization

On September 12, 1942, Charles A. McCall received a certificate of completion for 390 course work hours in "Theory and Practice of Diesel Engine Operation" from the Ohio State University "ENGINEERING, SCIENCE, AND MANAGEMENT WAR TRAINING PROGRAM." Once again Grandpa Charlie headed home to the mountains of North Carolina and the bosom of his family. I wonder if he and Grandma Delphie both felt this time together would be the last for a painfully long period, and I think they probably did share that unspoken fear. But, as he had written to her, "there is a war to be fought . . . so I guess I'll have to move along."

Ensign McCall reported to the U.S. Navy Amphibious Base at Little Creek, Virginia on September 22, 1942, for commando training. As he describes his experience there, it sounds somewhat like that of the Navy Seals today. Grandpa Charlie was about to be toughened up even more; he was also, eventually, heading for the hospital.

The following letters from Little Creek and the U.S. Naval Hospital were written by Grandpa Charlie during the last quarter of 1942.

Norfolk, Virginia
September 23, 1942

Dear Mama,

Had a nice trip and arrived safely and on time. I am very displeased with this as a place to stay but will not have to put up with it long since I am shoving off tomorrow.

When I reported yesterday the officer-in-charge told me that I would leave here Thursday morning for Solomons Island and I got quite a thrill but he went on to say "Solomons Island, Maryland" which is a training base just below Baltimore. I will be there about eight weeks for some extensive physical training and practice in the work I am taking up.

If you haven't already sent my cruise box hold it until I send you my new address. If you have already sent it—let me know by special delivery—c/o Commander Amphibious Forces, Naval Operating Base, Norfolk, Va.

Will write again and give you my address as soon as I am located.

Love,
Charles

U.S.N. Amphibious Base
Little Creek, Virginia
September 26, 1942

Dear Mama,

I finally located some paper and have a few minutes time so I'll try to tell you something about myself. I am so mixed up from all this moving around I have done the last few days that I am not sure I can write anything very clearly.

I was at Norfolk two days, came here for a few hours and went from here to Dam Neck where I had two days training and practice in anti-aircraft gunnery. I came back here last night and learned just a few minutes ago that I will probably be here three weeks for training in landing boat maneuvers and invasion tactics. From here I go to Solomans Island, Maryland for further training (unless there is a change in plans which seems to be quite common these days).

This training seems to be plenty tough but not any tougher, I suppose than the job we have to do. It is very interesting and very good physical training if you can take it.

I will not be paid until the first but am making it fine. I will not be able to send money for my cruise box until then but if it is convenient and possible you might send it (express) to Norfolk with a note to "hold until called for." Whatever you do let me know as soon as possible.

Time's up so I'll close hoping to hear from you very soon.

Love,
Charles

P.S. I'm anxious to find out if the
suits fit the boys.

C

(September 26, 1942)
(postcard)

> ENS. C.A. McCall, USNR
> USN Amphibious Base
> Little Creek, VA.

Dear Mama,

I'll be here long enough for you to write me if you will do so right away and send it air mail. Let me know what has happened to my box and hold it until further notice if it is still there. You may open it and get the package addressed to you.

I am a commando now and undergoing some very strenuous training—night and day—but it is fun and I enjoy it. There is no stationery here or I would write more. You will hear from me soon.

Address Above

> Charles

U.S.N. Amphibious Base
Little Creek, Virginia
September 28, 1942

Dear Mama,

I haven't heard from you yet but considering how this place is so isolated and so far away from everywhere that isn't hard to understand. It is kind of lonesome here at times but I am kept so busy that I don't have much time to think of that.

I am beginning to feel the need of my cruise box now. Kaki is all that is worn around here on duty and with only one suit it is somewhat of a problem. Tom's box hasn't come yet either but he had a little more in his bag than I had and together we are making out—after a fashion.

I don't think that I told you about coming back to Brevard the Sunday night after I left. After going to Asheville I found out that I wouldn't be able to leave there until four o'clock the next afternoon and Wilkerson insisted that I come back and stay at her house so I did.

This place isn't so far from Newport News and I want to go down there the first chance I have to look up some of my old friends. Luther Ferguson (Burke's brother), Max Hannah and dozens of other people I know are down there. Liberty very seldom comes to us here, however, so I don't know when I'll get away.

I am living in the officers quarters here which are very nice but I had rather live in town because this way I don't draw the sixty dollars per month rental allowance. I could live out but there are no satisfactory places near here and the irregular hours I have will not permit me to stay very far away.

When you write will you send me Helen's address. I would like to write her and when I go up to Solomans Island I may have a chance to go over and see her.

Let me hear from you soon.

Love,
Charles

UNITED STATES NAVY

U. S. Amphibious Base
Little Creek, Virginia
October 1, 1942

Dear Mama,

Your letter came today and I was glad to hear from you and to learn that the box has been sent. I haven't had a chance to go over to Norfolk yet to get it but will do so right away.

I have been in bed the last two days with a terrible cold but I just about have it whipped and am ready to go back to work. I am teaching a class in mechanical engineering now two hours each morning in addition to my other duties which makes me even busier than before.

You should have opened the box and got the package but since you didn't I will send it just as soon as possible.

Give my regards to everyone and write often.

Love,
Charles

U. S. N. Amphibious Base
Little Creek, Virginia
October 1, 1942

Dear Mama,

    Your letter came today and I was glad to hear from you and to learn that the box has been sent. I haven't had a chance to go over to Norfolk yet to get it but will do so right away.

    I have been in bed the last two days with a terrible cold but I just about have it whipped and am ready to go back to work. I am teaching a class in mechanical engineering now two hours each morning in addition to my other duties which makes me even busier than before.

    You should have opened the box and got the package but since you didn't I will send it just as soon as possible.

    Give my regards to everyone and write often.

                            Love, Charles

UNITED STATE NAVY

U.S. N. Amphib Base
Little Creek, Virginia
October 5, 1942

Dear Daddy,

Received your wire today as well as a couple of letters from Mama concerning the cruise Box. Thanks a million for all the concern you have shown regarding the matter. I have sent to Norfolk for the box and expect it most any day. The time I have spent in this man's navy has taught me not to worry over small matters like that but let them take care of themselves. Thanks anyway for all the trouble you were put to.

What is the old proverb we hear about the "plans of mice & men." Well it seems that plans in the Navy are outlines of things never done. At least, I was told this morning that I am being kept here indefinitely as instructor of mechanical & electrical engineering and for some research work & experiment with a new engine the Navy is working on. I am not very well pleased with the assignment even if it is very complimentary but orders are orders so I suppose I will be here a while. (at least until there is another change in plans which, it seems, could come in five minutes.

Mama told me about the *wonderful* surprise you had when you received your check. I think the State of North Carolina should either disbandon their school system or else publicly proclaim themselves slave drivers or highway robbers.

I am not in any too good a condition myself right now because of several factors but realizing the condition you no doubt find yourself in I am sending you a twenty. Hope it will help some. Conditions normal I sincerely hope to be in a position to help you more before long. I am making some secret investments now which I hope will be beneficial to both of us later on.

Mama says she has received my life insurance policy. Do you understand its terms. Having never seen, it, all I know is what I was told when I purchased it. If I am clear on the matter—In case of death you would receive in a lump sum the amount of six months salary plus (depending upon the age of the beneficiary), in this case about $1200 which would make a total of around $2500 and monthly payments of around $95.00 until death or the amount of $10,000. Am I correct? I should like to know the exact terms if you will let me hear from you.

How is everyone. Write soon and please don't fail to call on me if you need any help.

Have you been squirrel hunting?

Your
Chas. A.

UNITED STATES NAVY

U.S.N. Amphib. Base
Little Creek, Virginia
Tuesday
(October 7, 1942)

Dear Mama,

Just a word to let you know that I have received my cruise box and everything is O.K. I am mailing the package and you should receive it very soon.

I had week-end liberty (Saturday noon until Monday morning) this past week and went over to Newport News. Had a very enjoyable visit with lots of old friends. Saw Max, Luther Ferguson, and dozens of other people I knew. The most interesting thing of the whole week-end was the trip over there. The captain of the ferry was an old man (76) and a direct descendant of George Washington. He invited me up on the bridge of the ship and we passed over the site of the battle of the 'Moniter & the Merrimac." He steered several miles out of his way to explain the exact conditions of the battle and didn't leave out a single detail. Very interesting.

How are all the kids? And how is Jerry getting along in school? Give them my regards. You haven't sent Helen's address yet.

Sally is coming over this week-end if I can get off so you see I am not having "all work" even though it seems that way at times. Tom is still here and probably will be for some time.

Best wishes to you all.

Love,
Charles

P.S. Very glad to hear that the insurance policy arrived.

WESTERN
UNION

Newport News Vir 526pm 10-10-42

Mrs Clyde S. Mccall   Toxaway

Missing you today very much. Wish I were there, love

Charles

840 am

We Are not open on Sunday, ...

U.S.N. Amphibious Base
Little Creek, Virginia
October 14, 1942

Dear Mama,

Haven't heard from you in several days now. The paper came yesterday.

I am leaving here probably tomorrow or next day. I am going up to Solomans Island as an instructor in the advanced school there. At least, that is my orders but I have an idea that I'll be sent to a ship before long.

Have you received the candy and the package? I sent the telegram Sunday afternoon when I had a few hours off and was feeling a little love.

The weather here has really been foul for the past few days. It has been raining constantly and a strong wind blowing. Suppose it will turn cold after this.

I had a letter from Helen today. She seems to be getting along fine. I hope I will be able to get over to see her but it looks rather doubtful now since all liberty for officers has been stopped and it looks like I will be on the job twenty four hours a day seven days a week.

Tom is staying here and it looks like we are going to be separated for the first time.

Will send you my address as soon as I get there.

Let me hear from you soon.

Love,
Charles

UNITED STATES NAVY

U.S.N. Amphibious B.
Little Creek, Virginia
October 23, 1942

Dear Mama,

I am still here at Little Creek and don't know any more about leaving than I did the last time I wrote. I may be here several weeks yet and then I might leave tomorrow.

It has been raining a lot here the past week but it is clear now and the sun is almost hot as summer time. This is a new base here and the rain makes it awfully muddy and sloppy.

The apples came and were very good.

Has the package arrived yet. I am very anxious to find out whether or not the boys suits fit them. I can arrange a change if they don't.

Let me hear from you soon.

Love,
Charles

P.S. I am getting Ducky something if I can ever arrange to get to town before the stores close. I only get away from here about once a week now and then only from seven to twelve.
I would like you to send me a Kodak size group picture of Jerry and Dan if you can get one.

C

U.S.N. Amphibious Base
Little Creek, Virginia
November 11, 1942

Dear Mama,

I haven't heard from you now in over a week. The paper came the other day but no letter. I sure miss hearing from you.

Helen has written me since I last wrote you. She seems to be doing fine. I haven't had a chance to get up there to see her yet and don't see much hope of going at all. I sure would like to get up that way for a week-end. Pettit is working in Washington now for the Treasury department and I would like to see her.

How are things down there now? I suppose Winter has come. It is rather cold here. I have bought myself some long underwear and a pair of boots in preparation for it. I stay out at sea some nights until midnight or after and it really gets cold.

How is Doris. I imagine John is having quite a struggle making ends meet with the hospital bill, etc. How is he making out?

Sally was down a few days ago for the week-end. I was not able to see her very much but we had a very enjoyable time while we were together.

How is Grandpa McCall? I sure would like to see him and talk to him. I promised to write Grandma Owen but haven't done so yet.

Give the kids my regards—sure would like to see them. Write soon.

Love,
Charles

U.S.S.LCI (L) 209
c/o Postmaster
New York
(Nov. 14, 1942)

Dear Mama,

Things were going along normally until this morning at eight thirty when I was given orders to report to this ship immediately. I came aboard about eleven o'clock and reported for duty. We are underway tonight and moving right along.

I'll try to tell you a few things if this gets by the censor. First—I'm not going any place far away soon. I will let you know before I do. This is a rather large ship and very nice. I am engineering officer, have a private state-room and a wonderful set-up. I like this much better than any previous duty and will fare much better here than at Little Creek.

Write me real soon to the above address as I will probably get that sooner than any letter you have already written to little creek. I probably wouldn't get the paper but you might send some clippings in your letters.

Much love,
Charles

U.S.S. LCI (L) 209
c/o Postmaster, New York
November 16, 1942

Dear Mama,

It sure would be nice to hear from you. I haven't heard for over a week before I left Little Creek and I haven't been able to get any mail from there since I left. In fact, I haven't been ashore since coming aboard and no mail has been delivered to us.

I am liking this duty fine, the best yet. It is rather lonely out here but I am kept too busy to be bothered about that. We are under way twenty four hours per day and it keeps me pretty busy. I have two chief petty officers under me who are very good men, however, and I take time out now and then for a nap, leaving them in charge.

It is awfully cold out here at night. The quarters are nice & comfortable and so are the engine rooms but I have a bridge watch of four hours every night (In command of the ship—plotting courses, etc) and it's plenty cold up there.

Write often and don't worry about me. I'm perfectly safe and happy.

Love,
Charles

U.S.S. LCI (L) 209
c/o Postmaster, New York
November 21, 1942

Dear Mama,

Received your letter today. Sure was good to hear from you again.

I'm awfully sorry about Ducky's coat. I was afraid it would be too large and should have asked for her size before buying it. I did arrange to have it exchanged in case of a misfit, however, and that can be done very easily. I probably won't be back in Norfolk and if you can arrange the trade through the store it will be much easier, but if you have trouble let me know and I will write them myself. The store is one of the largest in Norfolk and has a name of being very reliable.

I had a letter from Sue. She seems to be very happy about her job and doing very well. She told me that John has been placed in classification 1-A. It is too bad that it has to be like that and a little unfair, I would say. I have advised him to join the Navy before he is called. Do you know what he is going to do? If he had come in about a month ago and had finished his initial training, I could get him on my ship right now since we have a vacancy in my Department which I must fill within a few days.

This finds me very well and happy. We are cruising along in formation "somewhere at sea" at twenty knots. The weather is beautiful but a rather strong Nort'easter plus some nasty ground swells is giving us a stiff roll which tends to slide me from bulkhead to starboard quarterdeck as I write. The odor of steak smothered in onions coming from the galley tells me that the mess attendant will be right in with my noon chow (It is served to me privately in my state-room) so I'll knock off for now.

Write soon.
Love,
Charles

U.S.S. LCI (L) 209
c/o Postmaster, New York
(Baltimore, MD
Nov. 27, 1942)

Dear Mama,

I suppose you have heard from Helen recently,

I am a little under the weather myself. I think I have a case of the flu plus a bad cough. Am going to a hospital tomorrow for a cure. It don't feel so awfully bad but the cough worries me, I have lost my appetite and can't smoke.

Outside of that I am fine.

I haven't heard from you lately. Will write more when I feel better.

Love,
Charles

U.S. Naval Hospital
Annapolis, Maryland
December 3, 1942

Dear Mama,

It seems that the little case of flu I had almost threw me and I was sent to the hospital here on the verge of pneumonia. It seems rather strange because I don't feel badly at all. Just a little weak and a little hoarse.

I hated to leave the ship because if I am here very long someone else may take my place and I will get a new job when I get out which I might not like as well. I suppose it is better that I am here, however, due to the circumstances.

It is very nice here and I get every attention possible. My meals are served to me in bed, my baths given me in bed, etc. so about all I have to do is sleep, read and rest.

I was rather worn out when I came and, believe me, I have been getting plenty of sleep. Please don't worry about me because I feel very good—no pain or discomfort at all and am in the very best hands to be found.

I received your letter containing the pictures and enjoyed them very much—exceptionally good, I think. Too bad about Ducky's coat, let me know if the proper amendments are made.

I was out to see Roy and Helen several times. That kid sure is a cute thing and growing like heck.

Doc says I will probably be here a couple of weeks so you may write to me here. Give everyone my regards and write often. Tell Daddy to write sometime.

Love,
Charles

U.S. Naval Hospital
Annapolis, Maryland
December 5, 1942

Dear Mama,

I'm feeling fine now. Wish I could get out of here but the Doc. still says two weeks. Seems that I'm some sort of miracle around here—I had pneumonia a week before I came here and went ahead with my work. I kept telling them that you can't kill a mountain hooger and they are beginning to believe me.

How is everyone there? Doubt if I'll get home for Christmas this time—sure wish I could.

I have a beautiful nurse but she just won't let me sit up long enough to write a letter. I do any way and she says I'm going to cause her to be fired yet.

Several fellows I know at the Academy have been over to see me, Pettit is coming tomorrow, I read a lot, and the time passes pretty good.

Write soon and don't worry. I'm doing fine.

Love,
Charles

U.S. Naval Hospital
Annapolis, Maryland
December 8, 1942

Dear Mama,

There really isn't anything much I can write about from here but since I know you are interested in hearing how I am getting along I will drop a note.

I really feel very good—like getting out and running—but I'm still confined to my bed. It is very lonesome here and with all the reading and sleeping I'm doing, I'm afraid I'm turning into quite a bad patient. There are some very nice nurses here and most of them don't seem to mind so much when every time they enter my door they are met with a barrage of paper-wads from some rubber bands I have hid away, etc. There is one old lady, however, about forty who is very dignified and won't even let me twist her ears without getting mad. Yesterday I had to go all the way over to the other side of the hospital for some xrays and the Doctor sent her in to push me over in a wheel chair (as if I couldn't walk). Well, the fun started. I told her "Lets play automobile" and started out like Dan crossing the front porch, blowing my horn at every turn. She started fussing and I fussed back about her back-seat driving. She was so embarrassed she didn't know which way to turn. On the way over we passed the Captain's office and I had quiet down a little but just beyond it was a sharp decline in the hall-way, waxed and very slick. It was all she could do to keep the chair from running away and about half-way down her feet flew up and her "what she sits down on" met the deck with a solid thud. She screamed and I laughed and the Captain, coming out to see what the trouble was, had a good laugh too. Well, it ended up with her being put to bed with some fractures and me honestly hoping to get out before she does to avoid a dose of poison or something.

That probably all sounds very silly to you but shows that I do feel good and have a little entertainment in spite of conditions.

How is everyone there? I haven't had a letter from you since coming here but suppose one is on the way.

The Doctor still contends that I can't get out under two weeks so I may as well settle down for some more rest. Write often.

Love,
Charles A.

U.S. Naval Hospital
Annapolis, Maryland
December 14, 1942

Dear Mama,

Had three letters from you one day last week. Two of them had been forwarded from my ship and the other sent directly here. Sure was glad to hear from you but it seems that one letter is missing somewhere in the chain. The letter mailed to me here said something about Joe Ben being much better and I hadn't even learned that he was sick. What was his trouble?

I am feeling fine, in fact the Doctor says that I am sufficiently recuperated to return to my ship but I must await orders which may be a week or longer coming through.

Had a very pleasant day yesterday. Sally called me from Columbus in the morning and Pettit came just after lunch and stayed until about seven o'clock. Bob McCall, the Midshipman I have told you about, has been coming over almost every afternoon and was here again last night.

I'm having quite a bit of trouble with my pay account. It seems that the pay master at Little Creek made some error in closing them out which necessitates my sending them back there for correction before I can be paid here. This, much to my regret, may cause a rather late delivery of any Christmas presents I may be able to send. The cost of my staying here at the Hospital, even though it consists only of my meals which is less than a dollar a day plus the fact that I must be prepared to pay for transportation back to my ship, the location of which is most uncertain, just about consumes what little available reserve I had laid away. Even at that I consider myself very fortunate to have a job which permits me to stay in one of the finest hospitals for only a few cents a day and at the same time draw my regular salary.

The paper came and I enjoyed it greatly. It seems that you never write any more about community news which is probably explained by the fact that there isn't any. I should like to know if T.C. McCall is still at State College and how he is getting along. Also about M.O. & J.B.

Sure am going to miss being home for Christmas this year. Don't know exactly where I will be but can't see any possibility of getting off. Hope all of you have a nice time.

It's awfully cold here this morning. Someone told me that the temperature was down around eighteen. We have had a couple of small snows during the last week but they didn't last very long.

Well, the war situation is beginning to look much brighter and for the first time since it's outbreak I am able to actually see its being over and lay some definite and concrete plans for that time. The time is many months away but still there is no doubt about its coming.

Love to all of you
Charles A.

4

Sure am going to miss being home for christmas this year. Don't know exactly where I will be but can't see any possibility of getting off. Hope all of you have a nice time.

It's awfully cold here this morning. Someone told me that the temperature was down around eighteen. We have had a couple of small snows during the last week but they didn't last very long.

Well, the war situation is beginning to look much brighter and for the first time since its outbreak I am able to actually see its being over and lay some definite and concrete plans for that time. She time is many months away but still there is no doubt about its coming.

Love to all of you
Charles

Ensign Charles A. McCall
US Naval Hospital
Annapolis, Maryland

U.S. Naval Hospital
Annapolis, Maryland
December 16, 1942

Dear Mama,

I'm feeling good but getting a little restless. The Doctor let me dress and go outside for a walk yesterday which was a great help. I noticed that I'm still a little weak and short-winded, probably due to lack of exercise.

I had a letter from my Commanding Officer yesterday and he is expecting me back. I was very glad to hear that because I didn't know whether they were gone away or not. If my orders come through within the next few days I think everything will be O.K.

Thanks for the letters and to Daddy & Ducky for theirs.

Love,
Charles A.

CHAPTER SEVEN

LCI(L)-42 and North Africa

From *Time* magazine, October 4, 1943: "One of the great U.S. building jobs in World War II was the high-speed constructions of the swarming fleets of landing craft for the Allied amphibious attacks on Sicily, Italy . . . the Navy had the task of turning out these clumsy, homely, efficient invasion boats by the thousands. It had to be in a tearing hurry with the greatest possible secrecy. . . . British studies revealed the need for an extra big troop landing boat; to meet the need the big LCI-L (Landing Craft, Infantry-Large) was developed. . . . The LCI-L, the only other vessel of the group able to navigate by itself on the high seas, is 155 ft. long and can carry about 200 infantrymen in an attack. Its crew and command are similar to those of the LST; officers and men on both develop esprit de corps, become inordinately fond of their strange craft, and look with pained incredulity on . . . civilians who consider their ships something less than . . . yachtlike." The day after Christmas, 1942, the Navy ship, USS LCI(L)-42 was commissioned. According to Naval Archives this ship had a 75 ton cargo capacity and was equipped with four single 20mm guns. With a fuel capacity of 110 tons, the LCI(L) could travel 4,000 miles at 12 knots, loaded. "She" had a complement of 2 officers and 21 enlisted men. Your Grandpa Charlie was destined to become one of those two officers. It is now January, 1943, and Ensign Charles Allen McCall will soon sail with his LCI(L)-42 crew from Little Creek, Virginia south to Bermuda and across the embattled Atlantic, on which they have already seen action, toward North Africa. The letters that follow chronicle Grandpa Charlie's first six months of duty in World War II.

January 5, 1943

Dear Mama,

Haven't had any mail for some time now but will drop you a line to let you know everything is O.K.

Had some pictures made a couple of days ago and I think they stink. Am sending you one anyway and hope you will find at least a bit of resemblance—I can't.

The last Brevard paper I received had a small article about Jim Galloway, Ransom's son, said he was a captain in the Army and told of his position. I knew where he was probably located and a few days ago I landed there. Day before yesterday I looked him up, spent the afternoon and had supper with him. He came to the ship yesterday and had supper with me. He is an awfully nice fellow big (about 6'2") and very nice looking. We get along nicely so I should have an enjoyable stay here. He is a rather influential person hereabouts—he expects a promotion to Major soon. Do you remember him? He says he remembers you and Daddy—that he saw Daddy on his last trip down there some five or six years ago.

How is everyone at home? Hope it isn't too cold and that everyone is well. Let me hear from you often.

Love to all
Charles

(postcard, THE EMERSON HOTEL
Room 623
Baltimore, MD
January 7, 1943)

Dear Mama,

Hope you got my letter. Very anxious to hear from you.

Everything is O.K. Will be here two weeks or longer. How's Dan?

Love,
Chas.

(January 8, 1943)

ADELPHIA HOTEL

CHESTNUT STREET AT THIRTEENTH
NEAREST EVERYTHING

PHILADELPHIA, PA.

Room 522

Dear Mama,

Just got here and will be here for two or three days. Haven't heard from you yet but will be looking for a letter when I get back to the Hotel in Baltimore.

Called Helen just before I left Baltimore & she says that Dan is much better. Very glad to hear it.

Getting along fair—working hard.

Love,
Charles

WESTERN
UNION

1943 JAN 21 AM 6 49

WASHINGTON DC

MRS CLYDE S MCCALL

   MISSION HOSPITAL ASHEVILLE NCAR

SHOVING OFF IMMEDIATELY. HOW IS DAN. WIRE COLLECT
WESTERNUNION

CHARLES

WESTERN UNION

1201

A. N. WILLIAMS
PRESIDENT

NEWCOMB CARLTON
CHAIRMAN OF THE BOARD

J. C. WILLEVER
FIRST VICE-PRESIDENT

The filing time shown in the date line on telegrams and day letters is STANDARD TIME at point of origin. Time of receipt is STANDARD TIME at point of destination

CFA19 6/9 NL=U WASHINGTON DC 20

BH5 JAN 21 AM 6 49

MRS CLYDE S MCCALL=

MISSION HOSPITAL ASHEVILLE NCAR=

SHOVING OFF IMMEDIATELY. HOW IS DAN. WIRE COLLECT
WESTERNUNION=

CHARLES.

(January 25, 1943)

THE
EMERSON

BALTIMORE, M.D.

Thursday Night

Dear Mama,

A change of plans will keep me here until the first of the week. Your letter came today and I sure was glad to hear that Dan is better. Don't worry about getting him home. It's much better for him there and would probably be cheaper than taking him home before he is ready.

I'm working awfully hard but feel good. My address will be U.S.S. LCI (L) 42, c/o Postmaster, New York. Write often.

Love,
Charles

U.S.S. LCI (L) 42
c/o Postmaster, N.Y.
January 31, 1943

Dear Mama,

Your letter reached me today. I was very glad to hear from you and to learn that Dan is at last on the road to recovery. Give him my regards and best wishes.

I left Baltimore on a moment's notice and was unable to go by and say good-bye to Helen.

I am feeling very good—gaining my weight back and working awfully hard. Don't worry about me and don't expect to hear from me very often.

Write often and give my regards to everyone.

Love,
Charles

U.S.S. LCI (L) 42
c/o Postmaster, New York
Feb. 10, 1943

Dear Mama,

Haven't heard from you in several days. Anxious to know how Dan and everyone is.

I'm well and happy—working hard and enjoying it greatly.

I really feel concerned about the length of my letters lately. I'm so absorbed in my work that I hardly have time to think of anything else and when I sit down to write I just can't find anything to say that would be of interest to you. My work for the last few weeks has been exceptionally hard because I have a new ship and almost an entirely green crew. I'm breaking them in fast and my work will gradually get lighter as I get them trained.

Regards to everyone.

Love,
Charles

UNITED STATES NAVY

February 15, 1943

Dear Mama,

Still no mail. I think this is the longest we've gone without it since just after we left the U.S. Perhaps it will come soon.

I sometimes wonder if you have trouble reading my letters. I don't know what it is but something terrible has happened to my handwriting. I can't even read it myself sometimes. Everyone else says they have the same trouble so I guess it's lack of practice some slightly "skaky" nerves now and then.

I saw Tom last night for the first time in several weeks. He says everything is O.K. back home,

For lack of something more interesting to write about, I'll tell something about some of the silly little suspicions and idiosyncrysies I have picked up over here. It's rather funny how important the little insignificant little things can seem to you under these conditions. For instance, I have a pair of "good luck" shoes. They're just a worn out old pair of brown slippers I bought while I was down in Charleston but I wouldn't take anything for them now. I started wearing them into action because they were old and loose, without strings, and would be easy to kick off if I had to hit the water. Now I wouldn't think of heading for danger without them on. They've brought me plenty of good luck so far.

Another thing that isn't so silly but just as strange was started by two friends and I just after we got over here without any particular reason at all. These old countries are very religious you know, mostly Catholic and the streets are always full of nuns, monks, etc. soliciting funds for the churches. Each time one of them approached me I give him a dollar. It's a very expensive habit but we tell ourselves that it brings luck—or—rather that not giving the dollar would bring bad luck. During one day of liberty not so long ago I gave away thirteen dollars. I guess that altogether I have given them over a hundred dollars but it's been worth that much. Somehow or other you get to putting a lot of faith in little things like that and it's very consoling.

There are many other things just as silly which I needn't tell about. Guess you get the idea.

The Skipper is being sent home pretty soon and they want me to take command of the ship but I don't want it. I want to remain in the engineering line if I can. Hope they don't force the job on me. I rank the executive officer, however, by almost a year and it would be a peculiar situation for him to be in command.

Guess I'd better close and get some sleep. Hope everyone at home is O.K. Love to all.

Yours,
Charles

(PASSED BY NAVAL CENSOR)

ENGINEERING OFFICER
U.S.S. LCI (L) No. 42
Feb. 18 1943

Dear Mama,

Haven't heard from you in weeks—did get a letter from you yesterday but it was written December 21. I'm very anxious to hear from Dan and the rest of you but will just have to wait and hope for the best.

How is the weather there now. It's about time for Spring and I'm going to miss the hills when the leave start turning green. Sure will be good for Dan when he can get out in the sun and run around.

Haven't heard from Helen since I left there. Today is her birthday and I haven't sent her even a card.

I'm getting along fine now. My work is getting a little easier now and I'm getting enough sleep, getting a sun tan, and feel fine. The sea is good for me and I'm learning to love it more every day.

I haven't heard from John and haven't written to him. I want to write to him soon so please send his address when you write next. How is he getting along.

Ducky and Jerry haven't written to me recently. Give Joe Ben and Dan my regards and tell Sue to write to me. How's Daddy?

Much love to All of You,

Charles.

(PASSED BY NAVAL CENSOR)
(FEB 25, 1943)

> U.S.S. LCI (L) #42
> Amphibious Post Office, N.O.B.
> Norfolk, Virginia

Dear Mama,

Had a letter from you a few days ago. Glad to hear that everyone is getting along nicely. Had a letter from Helen the same day and she says Dan already has the tube removed. Is that correct?

I got ashore Sunday night and tried to call Pettit only to find that she had been rushed to the hospital that afternoon with a case of acute appendicitis. I have been awfully worried about her but got a wire today saying she was coming along nicely.

I haven't been paid since I sent the last money and am not in a position to send any more. We don't have a paymaster aboard and have to wait until we dock long enough for our accounts to be taken up.

Regards to everyone.

> Love,
> Charles

(PASSED BY NAVAL CENSORS)

> U.S.S. LCI (L) #42
> c/o Amphibious Post Office
> N.O.B., Norfolk, Virginia
> March 7, 1943

Dear Mama,

I have been unusually busy for the past few days and haven't found time to write. I'm feeling good and getting along fine. Your and Dan's letters reached me yesterday and I sure enjoyed your nice long letter and it's fine to learn that Dan is finally about well.

I had last week-end off and went to Washington to see Pettit. I didn't get there until a little late Saturday night and couldn't see her then and since visiting hours at the hospital didn't begin until three-thirty Sunday afternoon I was afraid I wouldn't be able to see her at all but they let me in at eleven and I stayed until two. Her mother and Dad were in town and I went by to see them for just a few minutes. Mrs. Pettit said she would give you the message that I'm O.K. and anxious to get home. She is still in Washington but is going to take Alice home day after tomorrow.

Had a letter from John a few days ago. He seems to be O.K. in every respect. I have written a letter to him but since you say his address has been changed, I'll hold it until you send the new one since it will probably reach him sooner that way. Had a letter from Grandpa Owen and the family today.

I haven't written to Helen in several weeks. Give her my regards when you write. Sure hope she gets home for a while this Summer.

Haven't been paid yet and have about $200 income tax to pay when I do. Will send you some, however, if and when I get it.

Regards and best wishes to everyone. Write often.

> Love,
> Charles

Greenville, S.C.
March 9, 1943
9:30 p.m.

Dear Mrs. McCall,

Here we sit, my two best friends and I, eating peanut brittle candy and talking about food. I've just finished telling them about the wonderful supper we had at your house the night Charles brought me in rather unexpectedly. Hayne and Frannie (my two girl friends) are all for going to your house right now. Don't worry though, for it's a bit too far for us to walk at this hour of the night.

All joking aside, I do want to come up to see you sometime really soon when I am home. I've been planning to come ever since Christmas holidays, but school has kept me so busy. I don't want you to think the only reason I came to see you was to get the picture of Charles. Of course I did want it very much, but I also enjoyed your company a great deal.

I am glad that Dan is getting along so well now. I left the magazines (funny books) for Dan. I do hope Mother gave them to him.

I have several more now. I am going home for the day Sunday and I will leave them with Mother then.

They have moved the 100 boys still in school here into one wing of their dormitory and are making the rest of the building over for the aviation cadets. They are also building an obstacle course and some new barracks. As soon as school is out they will turn this dormitory over to the cadets; so I don't guess there will be any girls living on this campus next year.

I met a Lt. (junior grade) here yesterday who knew Charles in Norfolk. We got to talking and he said that he didn't know Charles as well as he would like to but that Charles certainly is one fine person.

It's getting late and I have a few things to wash out, before I go to bed; so I'll close for this time.

Love,
Bert

V - MAIL

Ensign Charles A. McCall
U.S.S. LCI (L) #42
c/o Fleet Post Office
New York, N.Y.

March 19 1943

Dear Mama,

Sorry I've waited so long to write but I'm *very* busy and I haven't heard from you in over two weeks.

I'm well, safe, happy, and having lots of fun. There are dozens of things I would like to tell you but for many reasons am unable to do so. Will be seeing you again, anyway, in a few months. Please don't worry too much about me—this is what I've been waiting for, in fact, living for for months now and I couldn't be happier. Just keep your fingers crossed and don't let those fryers grow too fast.

I'm the proud possessor of two campaign medals now—sure look good.

Please write often and let me know how everyone is. Regards to all.

love,
Charles

V - MAIL
PASSED BY NAVAL CENSORS

Ens. C.A. McCall
U.S.S. LCI (L) #42
c/o Fleet Post Office
NEW YORK, N.Y.
March 20 1943

Dear Mama,

    Have a chance to drop you a line if I do it in a hurry. We've been in a storm for the last two days and it's really been rugged. I've been on duty forty hours out of the last forty eight and am pretty tired but happy. Its lots of fun if you don't get sick or afraid. My mess attendant summed up the situation pretty well this morning. He is a young negro about seventeen and when I came down to my room this morning for a cup of coffee he was sitting on the deck shining my shoes—I've never seen anyone look as bad—he rolled his eyes once or twice & said "Suh! I didn't know the sea could be this mean" I enjoy it more than anything except for the fact that it gets too rough to cook and cold sandwiches get pretty old. I'm going to get some rest now. I'm safe & happy.

Love,
Charles

Bermuda
Postcard
No date or postmark

Mrs. Clyde S. McCall
Lake Toxaway,
North Carolina

Sure is a beautiful place. Forget this card.

No signature

Sure a beautiful
place. Forget this
card.

240—YANKEE STORE, BERMUDA

POST CARD

Mrs. Clyde S. McCall
Lake Toxaway,
North Carolina

Ye Towne of St. George's, Bermuda

Bermuda
Postcard
No date or postmark

Miss Alice Pettit
1815 Minnesota Ave., S.E.
Washington, D.C.

Hi, Angel,

It's really beautiful. I'm not sure now if it will be here or Texas—still your choice, however. This card is *just* for you.

With this full moon and Tropical climate—I'm slowly dying for lack of you.

Love always,
Charles

PASSED BY NAVAL CENSORS

U.S.S. LCI (L) 42

April 14, 1943*

Dear Mama,

Suppose you are rather worried about me since I haven't been able to write for some time. It's too bad I can't write more often but it's just one of those things that we have to accept as a result of what is going on. I assure you that I am perfectly well and happy. Please don't worry too much because it doesn't help matters at all.

I want you to write me at least twice a week and have the others write me. Letters sure do help (I suppose—I haven't had any in over a month now). I will write at every opportunity but sometimes that may be only once a month sometimes. I sure miss you and think about you lots. How is everyone? Is Dan well and have you heard from Helen? Where is John now? Is Sue still at Brevard? Did Grandpa Owen get better? How is Grandpa McCall?—give him my regards. How is the weather—are the trees green yet? How are Ducky and Jerry getting along in school? Tell Joe Ben Hello for me. Do you feel the rationing program very much? I saw eighteen hundred men yesterday who haven't had anything to eat but beans and corned beef for three weeks.

Well, hope this reaches you O.K. Love and regards to everyone—Tell Daddy to write to me.

*It's useless to worry
about where I am. Just
listen for the next big guns
and I'll probably be around.*

Always,
Chas. A. Moley

P.S. This will be mailed at the same time as a "V" mail written two or three days ago. I should like to know which reaches you first. If it is convenient, get some "V" mail to use in writing me.

*The day following Grandpa Charlie's arrival in North Africa, after a journey of over two weeks across the Atlanta Ocean.

lots. How is everyone? Is Dean well and have you heard from Helen? Where is John now? Is Sue still at Bernard? Did Grandpa Owen get better? How is Grandpa McCall? — give him my regards. How is the weather — are the trees green yet? How are Ducky and Jerry getting along in school? Tell Joe Ben hello for me. Do you feel the rationing program very much? — I saw eighteen hundred men yesterday who haven't had anything to eat but beans and corned beef for three weeks.

Well, hope this reaches you o.k. Love and regards to everyone — tell daddy to write to me.

it's useless to worry about where I am. just listen for the next big guns and I'll probably be around.

Always

Chas R. Mobley

P.S. This will be mailed at the same time as a "V" mail written two or three days ago. I should like to know which reaches you first. If it is convenient, get some "v" mail to

V---MAIL

PASSES BY NAVAL CENSORS

> Ens. Charles A. McCall
> U.S.S. LCI (L) #42
> c/o Fleet Post Office
> New York, N.Y.
> April 21, 1943

Dear Mama,

I suppose you would be interested to know that I have just learned I'm permitted to tell you where I am. Don't know how close you have guessed it but here it is—I'm somewhere in North Africa. That's about all I can say except that it's a long way from home. Very interesting and very exciting.

I was in Bermuda for a while and excepting none but perhaps Western North Carolina, it's the most beautiful place I have ever seen.

I haven't had any mail yet and am wondering how everything is back there. Sure would be nice to hear from you. How are my letters coming through? I have been writing two or three times a week.

Regards to everyone.

> Your loving son
> Charles

PASSED BY NAVAL CENSORS

V—MAIL

Ens. Charles A. McCall
U.S.S. LCI (L) #42
c/o Fleet Post Office
New York, N.Y.

April 28, 1943

Dear Mama,

The many tasks and duties that are facing me daily now makes time for writing pretty scarce but I will try to find that time at least every two or three days. After this is over I shall never say I can't find time for things any more. When you know that things must be done you just do them without worring about time.

I received my first letter from you yesterday. I think that it was dated March 19 but even at that it was like seeing the morning paper. Mail seems to be rather slow in coming through now but perhaps it will be better later on. Sure was glad to hear that everything was on an even keel at home.

There are a lot of things that I would like to tell you about North Africa such as the people and their habits, land, towns, etc. but all of that will have to wait until a later date. Several interesting things concerning the trip over also but that too will be delayed for a while. I ran into a soldier from Charlotte the other night and we sure had a lively discussion for a while. It seems that you have told me that "Mose" Whitmire was over here somewhere, is that true? If so, I would like for you to send me his adress and the address of anyone that is here. In all probability I will never have a chance to see any of them but if I should I would hate to miss it. It would really be fine to see someone from home around here. I suppose that if I had time, I would probably get a little homesick at times and worry about things back there but I don't have time to think about it which, I suppose, is vry good.

I am doing a pretty good job of collecting souvenirs, coins, etc. for all of you so if I am able to get back with them I think you will get a big kick from them. The one thing that I want worst is, and I think I am permitted to tell you about it, is this. They have these old street toilets here that you used to read about in Roman history. They are just shields that cover you from about your knees to your shoulders and while you are standing there doing your business (They are right on the edge of the sidewalk) you can watch the people go by and almost reach out and touch them. So what I want is a picture of myself in one of those with a crowd of women passing in front of me. We are not allowed to have cameras, however, so I haven't yet figured out how I will be able to get it.

You didn't say anything about John in your letter. Where is he now and how is he getting along. I don't have his new address so I wrote him a letter the other day and sent it there for you to forward. Did it arrive? When you write a letter try to squeeze in all the news that you can because they may not come for a month and some of them may be lost.

I suppose you will have a time with the kids when school is out. Give them all my love and tell Jerry to catch enough fish this summer for us both. What does Daddy plan to do this Summer. Sure hope he is able to find something suitable.

Do these come photographed or
Plain?   Love to everyone,

                                                            Charles Moley

PASSED BY NAVAL CENSORS

> (L.T. (J.g.) Charles A. McCall
> U.S.S. LCI (L) #42
> Fleet Post Office, N.Y.)

May 8, 1943

Dear Mama,

Am enclosing money orders for $125. Use the hundred as you see fit but keep the $25 for me, please. You know the way my pay accounts are always getting fouled up and since we are not being paid American money over here I might have to wire for it to come home on once I get back.

How is everyone? I am O.K. but hot weather sure is uncomfortable. Haven't heard from you in a good long while—guess the mail is fouled up somewhere.

Have a chance to see an old friend of mine if I make it snappy so will close for this time.

> Love to all
> Charles

P.S. Let me know as soon as
you receive this letter—mail
is rather uncertain, you know.

C

PASSED BY NAVAL CENSORS

(L.T. (J.G.) Charles A McCall
U.S.S.LCI (L) #42
Fleet Post Office
New York)

May 9, 1943

Dear Mama,

I think today is Mother's Day and the only way I have of sending my love and greetings is by a letter that will probably not reach you for two or three weeks. I do, however, send all my love and hope by this time next year I will be home again to celebrate the occasion.

I do have one present to send you and you'll never know how proud I am to send it. As you no doubt have already noticed by the address on the envelop—you may now write to me as Lt. (J.g.) Charles A. McCall. Yes, my promotion has finally come and I'm very happy about it. The (J.g.) is for junior grade. It corresponds to first lieutenant in the Army but doesn't sound quite as good, does it? And even worse than that, my next promotion will make me Lt. (senior grade) and if I were in the Army it would be captain. Oh well, I'm still glad I'm not in the Army.

I don't get a very great pay raise out of it—only about $20 a month but what makes me mad is that I'm loosing $96 a month by not being married. Even at that, however, I guess I'm not loosing much money. If I were married I would be drawing $301 per month which isn't bad at my age.

If you have one I want you to send me a small snapshot of Daddy. I have made handles for my .45 of the windshield of a Messerschmitt* and have a picture of my girl under one and would like his for the other. I sure have some stories to tell.

I haven't heard from you since I wrote last. Two letters is all I've had but I suppose that is pretty good considering the circumstances. I think I have a good idea about that—beginning with this one I am going to number my letters at the top beginning at (1) and the next one in succession (2), (3), (4), etc. If you will so the same then it will help both of us to get an idea of how the mail is coming through.

I remember a year ago today—I was home on my first leave. Sure would be nice to be there today but before that can be we have a little job to finish over here (which, by the way, is going pretty good right now, don't you think) and after that is over I'll see you again. Keep your fingers crossed.

Love to all
Lt. McCall

*German WWII fighter aircraft

V - MAIL

PASSED BY NAVAL CENSORS

> L.T. (Jg) Charles A. McCall
> U.S.S. LCI (L) #42
> Fleet Post Office, New York
> May 14, 1943

Dear Mama,

I wrote you the other day for the purpose of sending Mothers Day and birthday greetings but forgot about the birthday after I had started writing. Even if it is late—Happy birthday to you and Dan both. By the way, how is Dan now? You haven't mentioned him in your letters.

I am becoming more accustomed to life over here now and it isn't so bad after all, I suppose. Before it is over I guess the Mediterranean will be more or less a second home to me. If you can find any of our old French grammars I wish you would send me one. It's been so long since I studied it I'm very stale.

Your letter telling of Bert's marriage was news to me. I hadn't heard anything about it. Tell me more about it. Guess I won't have a car the next time I come home. Worry, Worry!

Is my mail coming through O.K.? I sure hope it is and also hope that you aren't worrying too much about me because everything is O.K. Please write often.

> Your loving Lt.
> Charles

provided. Use typewriter, dark ink, or pencil. Write plainly. Very small writing is not suitable.

No. 16163

Mrs Clyde S McCall
Lake Toxaway,
North Carolina

Lt. (j.g.) Charles A McCall
(Sender's name)
U.S.S. LCI(L) #42
(Sender's address)
Fleet Post Office, New York
May 14, 1945
(Date)

Dear Mama,

I wrote you the other day for the purpose of wishing mothers day and birthday greetings but forgot all about the birthday after I had started writing. Even if it is late, happy birthday to you and Clem too. By the way, how is Clem now? You never mentioned him in your letter.

I am becoming more accustomed to life over here now and it isn't so bad after all, I suppose. Before it is over I guess the Mediterranean will be more or less a second home to me. If you can find any of our old French grammars I wish you would send me one. It's been so long since I studied it I'm very stale.

Your letter telling of Dick's marriage was news to me I hadn't heard anything about it. Tell me more about it. Guess I won't have a car the next time I come home. Nory, Nory!

Is my mail coming through O.K.? I sure hope it is and also hope that you aren't worrying too much about me because everything is O.K. Please write often.

Your loving son
Charles

V-MAIL

PASSED BY NAVAL CENSORS

(U.S.S. LCI (L) No. 42)

May 21, 1943

Dear Mama,

Your letter of April 15 reached me a few days ago. Sure was glad to hear from you and to learn that everything is O.K. at home. You said that John was in South Dakota but you didn't give me his address. Please send it in your next letter. I suppose Helen will be very glad to get back home again. How long does she plan to stay?

What are the kids doing now that school is out? You'll have to put them to work in the garden. I sure am going to miss the "rostingears" (?) this year. Better have a whole half acre ready for me just in case I get back in time for them but I see very little hope of that.

Everything is fine with me. Something interesting is happening all the time and I enjoy seeing all the different places. Can't wait to have a look at Rome and Berlin.

Had a letter from Cullowhee the other day asking for payment of the remainder of my notes. I am prepared to send the whole amount if I can ever get to where I can get a money order. I think I can arrange that pretty soon.

Since there isn't much to say, I will close with love to all

Always
Charles

PASSED BY NAVAL CENSORS

CARTE POSTALE—Algerie
(POSTCARD—ALGERIA)

LT.(J.g.) Charles A. McCall

                              May 21, 1943

Dear Mama,

    Picked up several of these over here the other day. Gives you
some idea of how the people look.

    Am feeling fine but miss you all a lot.

                              Love,
                              Charles

7. - NEMOURS (Algérie). — Rue Gambetta et Hôtel de-Ville.

LT. (j.g.) Charles A. McCall

CARTE POSTALE S.

Dear Mama,

Picked up several of these over here the other day. Gives you a some idea of how the people look.

Am feeling fine but miss you all a lot.

Love,
Charles

Photolypie Etablis Photo-Albert, 5, Rue Rochambeau - Alger

MAY
21
1943
NAVY

Free

2 3¹ 5

Mrs. Clyde S. McCall

Lake Toxaway,

North Carolina

V-MAIL

PASSED BY NAVAL CENSORS

> Lt.(jg) Charles A. McCall
> U.S.S. LCI(L) No. 42
> Fleet Post Office, New York
> May 30, 1943

Dear Mama,

I haven't had a chance to write to you in several days—hope you haven't been too worried. I write as often as I can but sometimes, as you can well understand, it is impossible to get a letter out. My mail is coming through much better now. I had two "V mail" letters from Pettit the other day that were less than two weeks old. Yours are coming through O.K. too.

I saw Tom the other night and we really had one big happy reunion. I can't remember when I have been so glad to see anyone and we sure had a lot to talk about. He had a lot of news for me that I hadn't heard. One thing that one of our classmates, Charles McLaughlin, was killed in an airplane crash in Oklahoma a few weeks ago. He also had the picture and the article in the paper concerning Bert's marriage.

Just now got two letters from you dated May 8 and 12. Sure is nice to hear from you often. Me letters to you must be getting there in a hurry too since you had already heard that I am in North Africa.

We just got an official letter stating that our kaki uniform has been changed to one of slate tray. I am anxious to see them and get some but I suppose I won't have a chance to do that for some time. Tom had some very bad luck with his uniforms. He had his blues and whites stowed in a compartment that got flooded and ruined every one of them. Such things as that cannot be bought over here. I did manage to buy a set of Lt.(jg) shoulder boards from another officer and for the silver collar bars I used the very ingenious method of putting solder on a set of the gold ones I had. I'll give you the job of sewing the other stripe on my blues when I get back and until then in blues I'll just have to be a lowly Ensign.

I sent a money order to Cullowhee the other day paying in full the remainder of my notes. I think I will send you $125 as soon as I can get another money order. I would like for you to keep $25 for me in case I don't have any available when I get back.

Well, guess that's all for now. Keep writing and keep your fingers crossed.

Love to all
Charles

PASSED BY NAVAL CENSORS

U.S.S. LCI (L) 42

North Africa
June 13, 1943

Dear Mama,

Here it is Sunday morning but if it weren't for the calendar it might be any other day over here. I sure miss having a day off once in a while and going to church. The enemy, however, takes no holidays and if we are to keep up with them, we musn't take any either. Pearl Harbor was attached on a Sunday, you know. Just the same I am getting anxious for a few days rest and I have already decided that the first thing I am going to do after this war is over is come home and sit right flat on my "fanny" for a month.

You said something in one of your letters about the war in North Africa being over and expecting me home soon. Well, the war is over (on the land) but surely you can put two and two together and reach a better decision as to the time of my return since you know the type of ship I am on. In other words, the big job* is yet to come and all before this has been just a prelude. Didn't I mention something in a letter the other day about being anxious to visit certain places?

Yours and Ducky's letters giving Mose's address came and I have learned that he is some distance away but even at that I may see him sooner or later.

Everything is as well as usual with me. I have had a case of dysentery for a couple of days which has left me just a little weak. I feel much better today, however, and think everything will be O.K.

The mail has slowed down considerably but I get a letter now and then. Best regards to everyone.

Love,
Charles

*He is referring to the upcoming invasions of Sicily and Italy.

North Africa
June 13, 1943

Dear Mama,

Here it is Sunday morning but if it weren't for the calendar it might be any other day over here. I sure miss having a day off once in a while and going to church. The enemy, however, takes no holidays and if we are to keep up with them, we mustn't take any either. Pearl Harbor was attacked on a Sunday, you know. Just the same I am getting anxious for a few days rest and I have already decided that the first thing I am going to do after this war is over is come home and sit right flat on my "fanny" for a month.

You said something in one of your letters about the war in North Africa being over and expecting me home soon. Well, the war is over (on the land) but surely you can put two and two together and reach a better

V - MAIL

PASSED BY NAVAL CENSORS

U.S.S. LCI (L) 42

June 17, 1943

Dear Mama,

Just a few lines to let you know that everything is O.K. I had your letter the other day containing the pictures of Daddy and they are O.K. Thanks very much. The same day your letter came I had a letter from the Oak Grove Baptist Church. It was a form letter which they have evidently sent to all members in the service and was very nice. My mail in general has slowed down considerably but I get a letter now and then.

Things are as usual with me. I get a night off once in a while to go to town someplace but there is very little to do except look around. Sometimes I run into a cute little French girl and have a lot of fun understanding and being understood. Fundamentally, however, they are all the same—girls I mean.

Love always
Charles

Corpus Christi, Texas
June 17, 1943

Dear Mrs. McCall

    To begin with, you probably don't know me or never heard of me but I know your son Charles because I went to school with him, and just lately I heard he was in the Navy, well I too am In the Navy, and not having seen Charles for quiet some time I thought I'd write him and find out how he's getting along, however I don't have his address so I haven't been able to write before.

    If you would give me his address, I would like very much to write him.

My address is—

    Stephen W. Webb
      AMM 3/c U.S. NAVY
        Instructors School
         Rodd Field
           Corpus Christi, Texas

Thank You
Stephen Webb

P.S.
This is a flying field here.

(over)

I don't know if you still live at this address or not but I think it's right, as best I remember, anyway I hope so.

V - MAIL

PASSED BY NAVAL CENSORS

U.S.S. LCI (L) 42

June 25, 1943

Dear Mama,

The only trouble with the V-Mail is that by the time you get through filling in all the necessary addresses and return addresses you are already tired of writing. It's much easier to type them and I can get more in them that way but the typewriter is in use right now.

Have you received the letter containing the money orders yet? So many things could happen to a letter between here and there that I'm a little worried about it.

Your letter of June 4 reached me today. Sure was nice to hear from you—mail is rather scarce right now.

Every thing is about the same with me—plenty of work, lots of hot weather but it's all a lot of fun.

Love,
Charles

V - MAIL

PASSED BY NAVAL CENSORS

U.S.S. LCI (L) 42

June 28, 1943

Dear Mama,

Just a few words to let you know that everything is O.K. I haven't heard from you since I wrote last but that was only a couple of days ago so I suppose that everything is O.K. It takes a lot of the monotony out of things to get a letter now and then but when you can't get them you just have to do without.

You said in your last letter that Jerry had a letter from M.O. McCall. Maybe it isn't but it sounds kind of peculiar to me—Why should he write to Jerry? In another one of your letters several weeks ago you said that Tom had quit college—where is he now and what is he doing?

I keep hoping that I will run into someone from home around this vicinity but as yet I haven't seen a single person. I have seen dozens of fellows I was at the Academy with and some I have met elsewhere but none from around home unless you would cont Tom and I have only seen him once.

When the money orders I sent come through, I want you to subscribe to the Transylvania Times for me. I may not get a single copy of it and even if I do it will be several weeks old but just one copy would be worth the risk. Just have it sent to the address you use on your letters.

You mentioned something in one of your letters about not being able to send the book I asked for without a statement from my commanding officer. At the present time I don't need the book any more and don't want you to send it but I think Mr. Thomas is a little wrong about the matter. We have a copy of the order and unless it has been changed, it applies only to Army and Navy personell stationed ashore on foreign duty. Naval personell afloat or whose address is "Care of fleet Post Office" may still receive packages. See if that isn't correct and if it is I sure could go for a small box of candy. Of course, the Captain would write a dozen letters for me in a minute if I only asked him but I don't believe it is necessary unless the order has been changed and if it had been we would have been among the first notified of it. If you want to press the point which I don't advise, here is the essence of it all (1) My address is the same as it was when I was in the United States, (2) The movement of Naval vessels is ordinarly very secret in the strictest sense of the word, (3) The address of all Naval vessels in the Atlantic is the same as this one, ie "Care of Fleet Post Office, New York", whether they are in Africa, England, New York or Charleston, (4) How does Mr. Thomas know but what my ship is tie down to a dock in an American city for the duration—Maybe I am not and have never been out of the United States for all he knows. See what I mean. Oh well, guess I'm still a debator at heart.

Love to all,
Charles

CHAPTER EIGHT

Sicily and Salerno Invasions

T he Axis forces in North Africa surrendered to the Allies in mid May of 1943, turning over almost 300,000 prisoners. With the victory in North Africa secured, the Allied commanders immediately shifted focus to the invasion of Sicily, dubbed "Operation Husky." A tentative date for the invasion had been set for July 10 through July 14, this being the period for a favorable July moon. From late June through July 4th Allied forces carried out highly covert rehearsals for the upcoming assault landing. These drills were carried out under threat of discovery by German subs and fighter planes swarming the Mediterranean Sea. According to General Eisenhower's plan, ships of the Western Naval Task force commanded by United States Admiral Hewitt would convey General George Patton's Seventh Army to the shores of Sicily. On July 9, 1943, over six hundred ships and landing craft loaded with Patton's infantry soldiers headed for Sicily. Grandpa Charlie's LCI(L)-42 was in that convoy.

The following letters begin on July 4, 1943, just prior to the Sicilian invasion, continue throughout the summer and end with the Salerno landings in mid-September. So let's find out about Grandpa Charlie's Fourth of July sixty-seven years ago.

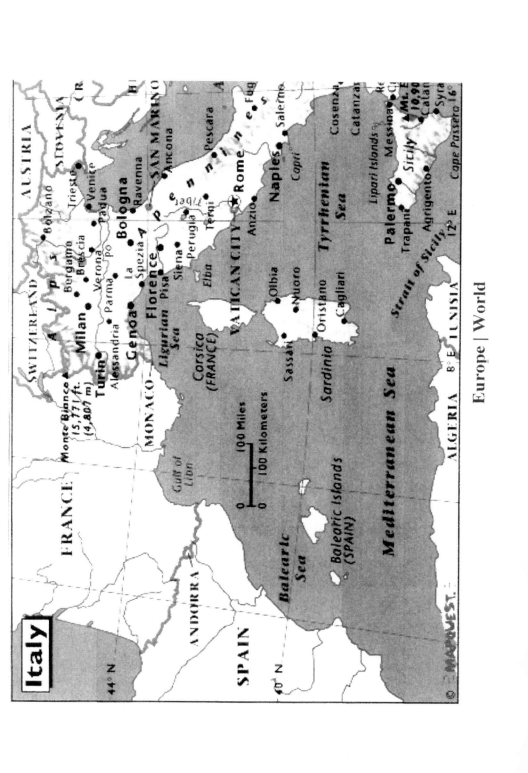

Italy

Europe | World

PASSED BY NAVAL CENSORS

U.S.S. LCI (L) No. 42

July 4, 1943

Dear Mama,

This is just about the strangest fourth of July I have ever gone through. I hope the next one is spent a little differently. I was home last year at this time, if you remember, on my way from Charleston to Columbus. The Navy life I was living at that time sure was different from the one I am living now but I believe, all in all, that I like this one better.

I don't imagine there was much celebration of the occasion around there, was there?

Every time I write I fine it just a little harder to think of anything to write about. I suppose that after a while all I can say will be just a repetition of what has gone before. Everything is fine with me as usual. As I am writing this my total uniform consists of one very small pair of shorts and as a result of wearing them for a good long while now I am as brown as a biscuit almost all over. I sleep out on deck every night and do quite a bit of swimming. I have worked most of my fat off but I am still pretty heavy.

Can't think of anything else to say except don't worry about me if you don't hear from me for a while.

Much love,
Charles

PASSED BY NAVAL CENSORS

U.S.S. LCI (L) No. 42

July 14, 1943

Dear Mama,

I suppose that along about now you are rather anxious to hear from me. I am glad to report that I am fine. A few times in my life I have thought I was tired but right now I can see where I was wrong. I'll tell you about it sometime but right now I have a chance to catch a short nap and, believe me, I'm taking it.

Don't know when I'll have a chance to mail this but it will reach you soon.

Love always,
Charles

P.S. Can't tell you where I am.*

*Sicilian occupation, July 9-15, 1943

July 14, 1943

Dear Mama,

I suppose that along about now you are rather anxious to hear from me. I am glad to report that I am fine. A few times in my life I have thought I was tired but right now I can see where I was wrong. I'll tell you about it sometime but right now I have a chance to catch a short nap and, believe me, I'm taking it.

Don't know when I'll have a chance to mail this but hope it will reach you soon.

Love always
Charles

P.S. can't tell you where I am.

PASSED BY NAVAL CENSORS

U.S.S. LCI (L) No. 42

July 17, 1943

Dear Mama,

Your letter of June 8 and the birthday card came today. Thanks a lot for the card, it's just about the nicest thing I have ever received.

I am fine, all rested up and feeling great. I had a day off yesterday and took advantage of it to get the feel of land again and to look around a bit. Sure had a good time.

On May 21 I sent $135 to Cullowhee which should have paid all my notes off. I haven't heard from them and am wondering if they have received it. Wish Daddy would write and find out. Also on June 9 I sent you $125—have you received that?

Nothing much to write now so will close. Let me hear from you often.

Love,
Charles

July 17, 1943

Dear Mama,

Your letter of June 8 and the birthday card came today. Thanks a lot for the card, it's just about the nicest thing I have ever received.

I am fine, all rested up and feeling great. I had a day off yesterday and took advantage of it to get the feel of land again and to look around a bit. Sure had a good time.

On May 21 I sent $135 to Cullowhee which should have paid all my notes off. I haven't heard from them and am wondering if they have received it. Wish Daddy would write and find out. Also on June 9 I sent you $125 - have you received that?

Nothing much to write now so will close. Let me hear from you often.
Love,
Charles

July 20, 1943

Dear Mama,

Well, it's been a great birthday. I haven't had anything to do all day so have just been sitting around reading. Went swimming for a while this afternoon. Sure hope I can spend my next one at home.

I still don't know anything more about when I'll get home than I did the first day I got here. I'll just have to wait and see, I guess. While eating supper tonight I got to thinking about how I could go for about six big ears of corn on the cob. We get fed pretty well but fresh vegetables are scarce and I sure miss them at this time of year. I am acting as commissary officer on the ship in addition to my other duties so I have cooked just what I want—that is of the things we have. I had a good cook up until a few days ago and after a little trouble with him I reduced his rate to apprentice seaman and got another one. The new one is learning fast but still can't fix everything just the way I want it. I like him, however, because he can make the most delicious corn bread you ever tasted. The other officers laugh at me and say our menu looks like one straight from a southern plantation.

I passed Tom at sea the other day but haven't seen him to talk to him except just the once I told you about. He is never very far away but always too far for me to see him.

Guess that's all for this time. Everything is O.K.

Love always,
Charles

PASSED BY NAVAL CENSORS

(CARTE POSTALE—TUNIS)
Postcard Tunisia

July 21, 1943

Suppose you've heard of this place rather often recently. Everything is O.K.

Charles

PASSED BY NAVAL CENSORS

U.S.S. LCI (L) No. 42

July 24, 1943

Dear Mama,

Even though there is very little to say, I haven't written for three or four days so will try to make a composition of some sort. I haven't heard from you for about a week but had a letter from Sue yesterday.

This business of Thomas not accepting packages for me has me rather agitated. The other fellows aboard ship receive packages regularly with no questions asked. If he would use a little common sense he would realize that my address is the same as it was when I was in the states and theoretically no one should know but what I am still there. I think he should study his regulations a little more thoroughly. I think the thing for you to do is to forget him and when you have something to mail take it to Brevard or some place where they know what is going on. And, for Pete's sake, don't mention the fact that I am on foreign duty—there is no reason at all why the postmaster should know that. As I have said before, I no longer want the French Grammer but sure would appreciate a good box of candy.

Things are progressing as usual with me. I have found the toughest part of the whole deal is the quiet days when nothing happens and you just sit and wait. At times like that you reason that you might just as well be at home and you can't understand why they don't put you to work, finish things up and send you back. Before I came into the service I used to wonder why it was always said that soldiers and sailors were always craving action; now I know. You realize that you have a certain job to do before you can go back to your normal life and the sooner it is done to better things are all the way around. Then, too, you have heard of the city man who couldn't sleep in the country because it was too quiet.

If you still get the Asheville paper I want you to do something for me. I would like for you to save all of them for me that have accounts of the major advances in this vicinity. To explain myself a little more thoroughly, I don't mean the daily advances of troops, etc. but such things as invasions, etc. It won't be such a job because there will probably be only a very few in which I will be interested. Do you understand what I mean?

I haven't received the Brevard paper you mailed yet. Some papers mailed that way do come through but I believe there is some regulation saying that papers may only be sent directly from the publishers. You might enclose some clippings for me in some of your letters.

Thanks for writing often and I will write at every opportunity. I can't see myself getting home any time soon.

Love to all,
Charles

U.S.S. LCI (L) No. 42

July 29, 1943

Dear Mama,

The Paper you mailed arrived yesterday in good condition. I certainly did enjoy reading it and thanks a lot for sending it. It was a little slow in coming through but even at that it was all news to me. I should appreciate your sending it often if it is convenient. I also had a letter from you yesterday which was written May 21 and one from Sue written July 3. Yours was ordinary mail and Sue's was V-mail. There seems to be a hitch in the mail some place because I have been getting very little the past month and that is taking much longer than it used to.

In your letter you asked about putting my picture in the paper. It is agreeable with me if you will limit any statement about my present duty to the following, "Attached to a vessel of the Navy Amphibious Forces somewhere in North Africa." At the present time that is all I am permitted to say and any addition would likely get me in "hot water." As for statements, I have none. I have been in the Navy since January of '42, spent four months as a Midshipman at the United States Naval Academy, three months at Ohio State University studying diesel and electrical engineering, and the remainder of the time I have been on sea duty. Anything concerning my life before the Navy is up to you. Oh yes, My promotion from Ensign to Lieutenant (junior grade) came on May 1.

I had a letter from John the other day and he seems to be doing fine. Has he heard anything more about getting his appointment to aviation cadet. I sure hope he can get it.

I was rather surprised to learn from Sue's letter that Helen had been home. I believe she said that they stayed a week. I imagine you were glad to see them. How do they seem to be getting along and how is Suzanne?

I am pretty busy today so until I can find more time I'll sign off.

Love to All
Charles

V - MAIL

PASSED BY NAVAL CENSORS

U.S.S. LCI (L) No. 42
August 1, 1943

Dear Mama,

It's nine thirty (early in the afternoon at Quebec) on Sunday night and I have just been sitting here for the last five minutes trying to remember what it was like to have Sunday off and just sit around and rest Sunday afternoon and Sunday night. When we are in port on Sundays we have church services on the deck of one of the ships or on the dock. That is usually from seven to seven thirty for protestants (six thirty to seven for Catholics) and other than that it is just another day.

Everything is fine with me as I hope it is at home. Haven't heard from you in some time. Love and best wishes to all.

Always
Charles

No. _____

Mrs. Clyde S. McCall
Lake Toxaway
North Carolina

Lt. (jg) Charles R. McCall
(Sender's name)
U.S.S. LCI(L) 46 42
(Sender's address)
Fleet Post Office, N.Y.

August 6, 1945
(Date)

Dear Mama,

It's nine thirty (early in the afternoon at Omaha) on Sunday night and I have just been sitting here for the last few minutes trying to remember what it was like to have Sunday off and just sit around and rest Sunday afternoon and Sunday night. When we are in port on Sundays we have church services on the dock or aboard the ships or on the dock. That is usually from seven to seven thirty for protestants (six thirty to seven for catholics) and other than that it is just another day.

Everything is fine with me and I hope it is at home. Haven't heard from you in some time. Love and best wishes to all.

Always,
Charles

V-MAIL

V - MAIL

PASSED BY NAVAL CENSORS

U.S.S. LCI (L) No. 42

August 4, 1943

Dear Mama,

Just as was beginning this I was surprised by a fellow coming in who was with me up in Columbus last Summer. That was seven o'clock and it is now twelve. We really had a good session talking over old times, friends, and experiences. You have no idea what a thrill it is to see an old friend over here so I really feel up in the clouds right now. This guy was a special friend anyway, about forty years old and with twenty years in the Navy.

Everything is fine with me except for the fact that no mail is coming through. Hope all of you are O.K.

Love
Charles

V - AIL

PASSED BY NAVAL CENSORS

U.S.S. LCI (L) No. 42

August 6, 1943

Dear Mama,

I have a little radio that I bought before leaving and now and then we get within range of an allied force station over here and I sure get a big kick out of listening to it. Most of the programs are rebroadcasts but they are good and the news comes directly from London twice each day. I just got today's news and it sounds pretty good. Sure will be glad when the little show is over.

Here it is the first of August and I'm not home yet. I guess I have been away from home longer now than I ever was before. Guess Christmas was the last time I was there.

Everything is fine. No mail for sometime.

Love,
Charles

V - MAIL

PASSED BY NAVAL CENSORS

U.S.S. LCI (L) No. 42

August 12, 1943

Dear Mama,

I had another stack of mail since I wrote you a couple of days ago. I think there were five or six letters from you and one from Daddy. Glad to know that everything is going well and hope that your mouth isn't giving you so much trouble by now. I am having a little trouble along that line myself—I have another wisdom tooth coming but it isn't nearly so bad as the other one was. I saw a dentist the other day and he said it was coming through nicely.

Was rather relieved to hear that you had received the money. I also had a letter from Cullowhee enclosing my old notes (believe I told you that before, didn't I?) Had a letter from Julius Tinsley which was a very pleasant surprise. It is hard to realize that his kid is two years old, makes me think that maybe I'm kind of getting behind. Had another letter from Sue written sometime the first of June and was late getting here because the address was incorrect. Several letters from Pettit and she is fine. Her mother and small brother had spent a week with her and her sister in Washington and she was thrilled pink over that. She has sent me a set of Lt.(jg) collar bars which I need badly and am looking forward to getting. Tell Ducky that the card she sent was as cute as a bug's ear and I thoroughly enjoyed it, especially the nice little notes she added.

There seems to be some doubt in your mind as to which type of mail is fastest. You know about my letters to you, of course, but on this end the time required is something like this—V-mail, ten days: air mail ten days to two weeks: ordinary mail, a month. I can easily see how it may be a different story on your end of the line so if you will let me know which is faster I shall adopt that type permanently.

I suppose by the time you get this that the kids will already have started to school and, as usual, you will be lost for several days without them. I am anxious to know how Dan gets along so let me know. If my guess is correct he will be kind of spoiled because of his long illness but that is to be expected and he may already be over that by now.

I want you to do something else for me. Take whatever amount of the money you have of mine that is necessary and subscribe to the Sunday Citizen for me. (Six months sub.) Be sure it is just the Sunday edition. I am getting more and more anxious for news and that should be a great help. I will let you know when the Transylvania Time begins coming.

Everything is fine here and I'm getting along good. Two years ago today I joined the Navy and have yet to regret it. Write often

Love,
Charles

PASSED BY NAVAL CENSORS

August 18, 1943

Dear Mama,

Your V-mail letter of July 31 came yesterday. Glad to know that everyone is getting along well. I am fine.

The French book and another Transylvania times arrived two or three days ago and thanks a lot for both of them. You sent the French reader instead of the French grammer but it will serve the purpose just about as well. Don't bother about sending cigarettes because they are plentiful and only cost me 4 ½ c per pack while you will have to pay 15c. If you want to send something, make it something to eat.

There's nothing much to write about so will close for now.

Love,
Charles

PASSED BY NAVAL CENSORS

U.S.S. LCI (L) No. 42

August 25, 1943

Dear Mama,

Haven't had an opportunity to write you for several days. Hope you haven't worried. I am fine and everything here about as usual so far as I am permitted to say.

Had several letters from you the other day—the most recent ones v-mails of August 4 & 5—one from Daddy on the 4th. Glad to know that everyone is O.K.

Yes, I have written to Mrs. Wilkerson. Not knowing Bert's new name or address and being desirous of sending her my best wishes for happiness, a note via the old lady was the simplest way out. Nice of her to call on you, I think.

Neighborhood gossip is gospel compared with the idle memos which float around concerning our homecoming. I know nothing and even if I did would be unable to tell you. I have settled myself for two years of foreign duty which is the usual schedule and if I get back before then it will just be luck. Since my promotion, I am holding a job below my rank which, unimportant as it is in wartime, may mean a transfer soon but even if that comes it will probably mean something else over here. I just hope I get back in time to get a crack at the Pacific before that show is over or else get on around there from here. I always dreamed of a trip around the world.

Guess that's all for now. Write often.

Love,
Charles

PASSED BY NAVAL CENSORS

U.S.S. LCI (L) No. 42

August 30, 1943

Dear Mama,

It seems to me that I'm rather young to be entering my second childhood but when that box of candy you sent came yesterday I could have sworn that I felt it coming on. Honestly, there was never a pepermint stick or chocolet drop that I enjoyed more. Thanks a million.

I have received two newspapers sent by you and the first one from the publisher came yesterday. It was the July 29 issue and I received it August 29 which is pretty good, I think. By the way, the picture on the front page and the articles concerning the invasion of Sicily were *very* interesting.

Everything is O.K. and I am fine. I'm looking forward to Fall and cool weather which you folks probably are already feeling.

Am enclosing a little item for Jerry if it gets by the censor. 1 franc = 2 c.

Love to all
Charles

PASSED BY NAVAL CENSORS

U.S.S. LCI (L) No. 42

August 31, 1943

Dear Jerry,

Your letter came yesterday. Sure was glad to hear from you.

Has school started yet and who is your Teacher? Do you have to study hard? I'll bet you make all "A's."

I wonder if you and Dan caught many fish this year or were they all minnows? I sure would like to get home and go fishing with you.

I see a lot of airplanes over here that you would like to see. The P-38's are the ones with double bodies back of the wings and they can really take off. They go so fast sometimes that they are hard to see. Do you know what the other name for a B-17 is? It is the Flying Fortress. I guess John sees lots of planes too, don't you, and rides them too. I ride them sometimes. I have seen lots of Messershmitt 109's and Junkers 88's. Do you know what they are?

The Navy is building a new kind of ship. They are called D.E.'s which stands for Destroyer Escorts. They are smaller than Destroyers. They are beautiful little ships and I would like to be on one of them. I can't tell you any more about them because it is a military secret.

What kind of Australian money did M.O. send you? Were they half-penney's, penneys, three pense, six pense, half crown's or crowns? I have a lot of coins for you including some from Italy and Germany but the censor will not let me send them through the mail.

I showed the Captain of my ship your letter and he said he would like to have you aboard as cabin boy. Would you like that or would you rather be the skipper yourself?

Write me again when you have time and be a good boy.

Your *little* brother,
Charles

August 31, 1943

Dear Jerry,

Your letter came yesterday. Sure was glad to hear from you.

Has school started yet and who is your Teacher? Do you have to study hard? I'll bet you make all "A's."

I wonder if you and Dan caught many fish this year or were they all minnows? I sure would like to get home and go fishing with you.

I see a lot of Airplanes over here that you would like to see. The P-38's are the ones with double bodies back of the wings and they can really take off. They go so fast sometimes that they are hard to see. Do you know what the other name for a B-17 is? It is the Flying Fortress. I guess John sees lots of planes too, don't you, and rides them too. I ride them sometimes. I have seen lots of Messershmitt 109's and Junkers 88's. Do you know what they are?

V - MAIL

PASSED BY NAVAL CENSORS

U.S.S. LCI (L) No. 42

Sept. 1, 1943

Dear Mama,

Here it is the first of September—time is really flying by. Guess the nights and early mornings there are beginning to get a little chilly and pretty soon a small fire in the fireplace will feel pretty good. The katydids have probably already started their nightly warnings of the inevitable events ahead and the cows spend more and more time chewing their cuds in the warm sunshine and grieving because the grass is no longer young and tender like it was a few months ago. Apples will be getting ripe soon and the yellow jackets and hornets will be so persistent in living their last few days with a full belly that they openly declare war against the coming process. How's that for something to write about—guess I should have been an author.*

All's well
Charles

* He was, don't you think.

PASSED BY NAVAL CENSORS

U.S.S. LCI (L) No. 42

September 14, 1943

Dear Mama,

I had a couple of letters from you yesterday the latest of which was August 17, I believe. Glad to know that everyone is well. Also had a letter from Sue.

There is some discussion in our group concerning how far censorship will let us go in telling of our recent activities. No one is sure so I will take a chance and tell you this. I had a *very* active part in the invasions of Sicily and Italy. That isn't for publication, definitely, and I think you will know how to treat it. You have probably already guessed this by putting two and two together so it shouldn't be news to you. That's my job, you know. I understand that the LCI's are receiving quite a bit of publicity back there now. Have you heard anything about us. A London paper carried a picture of this one (the 42) the other day which was taken on the beach at Sicily. We were once a more or less scout weapon but the Huns have got to know us *pretty* well now so we are beginning to be publicised.

I guess the news of Italy's collapse cheered you about as much as it did us. There is no time, however, because we are determined to drive the Hun down the same bloody road and, with the help of God, he'll soon be packing.

All's well with me as usual.

Love,
Charles

Haven't heard from John for some
Time. Has he been home?

September 14, 1943

Dear Mama,

I had a couple of letters from you yesterday the latest one of which was August 17, I believe. Glad to know that everyone is well. Also had a letter from Sue.

There is some discussion in our group concerning how much censorship will let us go in telling of our recent activities. No one is sure so I will take a chance and tell you this. I had a very active part in the invasions of Sicily and Italy. That isn't for publication, definitely, and I think you will know how to treat it. You have probably already guessed this by putting two and two together so it shouldn't be news to you. That's my job, you know. I understand

V - MAIL

PASSED BY NAVAL CENSORS

U.S.S. LCI (L) No. 42

(SEPT 18, 1943)

Dear Mama,

Because of the date and the news I thought you might be interested in hearing from me. Glad to report that all is well and I'm fine.

Haven't heard from you in sometime but haven't been able to get any mail for several days which, no doubt, explains that. Hope some of my letters are getting through. It sure would be interesting if I could tell you all my experiences as they occur but perhaps it is better that I can't. Some of these letters, however, might serve as leads to some interesting tales later on. Hold them.

Don't worry about me, everything is fine and after about ten or twelve more invasions I'm expecting some patrol duty in Sol's hanch.

Love always
Charles

To
Mrs. Clyde S. McCall
Lake Toxaway,
North Carolina

From
Lt.(jg) Charles A. McCall
(Sender's name)
USS LCI(L) No. 42
(Sender's address)
Fleet Post Office, N.Y.

(Date)

Dear Moma,

Because of the date and the news I thought you might be interested in hearing from me. Glad to report that all is well and I'm fine.

Haven't heard from you in some time but haven't been able to get any mail for several days which, no doubt, explains that. Hope some of my letters are getting through. It sure would be interesting if I could tell you all my experiences as they occur but perhaps it is better that I can't. Some of these letters, however, might serve as leads to some interesting tales later on. Hold them.

Don't worry about me, everything is fine and after about ten or twelve more missions I'm expecting some patrol duty in Sol's branch.

Your always
Charles

V---MAIL

PASSED BY NAVAL CENSORS

U.S.S. LCI (L) No. 42

September 18, 1943

Dear Mama,

I still hope you understand how at times it is impossible to get mail out. I haven't written for several days and that is the only reason. Everything is fine with me—hope it is the same with you folks.

I found a magazine article the other day which I thought might prove interesting to you. It is a little out of date but gives you some idea of my work and the outfit I'm in. The training program described is what I was going through with last Fall and Winter. The LCI pictured is identical to mine and I thought that might interest you.

I saw Tom again yesterday and we had quite a chat. He is fine and we are both looking forward to getting home again.

I just have time for a note if I am to get it into this mail. Will write more soon.

Love,
Chas.

—Official U. S. Navy Photograph.

Amphibious force in action: Army troops stream out of a LCI (Landing Craft: Infantry) during invasion maneuvers along Atlantic coast.

The 'Amphibs' Are Training to Strike

Unified Invasion Force, Composed of Picked Army and Navy Officers and Men, Getting Ready

At bases along both coasts of the United States, it can now be revealed, there is a unified force composed of picked Army and Navy officers and men being welded in preparation for assaults on enemy territory. These are the "Amphibians," (INFORMATION BULLETIN, May 1943, p. 6), upon whom will develop the task of carrying the fight to the enemy— starting the offensive on enemy-held shores.

On the Pacific coast, under Rear Admiral Francis W. Rockwell, U. S. Navy, commander Amphibious Force, Pacific Fleet, who personally directed the landing operations on Attu, and on the Atlantic coast, under Rear Admiral Alan G. Kirk, U. S. Navy, commander Amphibious Force, Atlantic Fleet, there has been created a striking force, still in process of expansion, ready to carry out with speed, precision, and perfect coordination the most difficult of military assignments—a landing on a fortified hostile shore.

Under the training courses of the Amphibious Forces, thousands of naval officers and men have learned to take the newly designed landing boats, ships, and amphibious craft through heavy surf safely to selected beaches; and thousands of toughened Army troops have learned to swarm ashore from the landing craft and race for the beach to establish the spearhead of an Allied invasion.

On the Atlantic coast, for instance, working together in the closest cooperation, especially selected Army and

Rear Admiral Alan G. Kirk

—Official U. S. Navy Photographs

Rear Admiral Francis W. Rockwell

PASSED BY NAVAL CENSORS

U.S.S. LCI (L) No. 42

September 23, 1943

Dear Mama,

Had a letter from you yesterday mailed August 14. Glad to hear everything is good with you.

Everything is fine with me and there is no need for worry. Love and best wishes to all

Charles

PASSED BY NAVAL CENSORS

(Post Card Palermo, Italy)
LT. (j.g.) Charles A. McCall, USNR

Sept. 23, 1943

    Sure have seen lots of interesting things but would like to see some a little more familiar now.

PASSED BY NAVAL CENSORS

(Post Card Palermo, Italy)
LT. (j.g.) Charles A. McCall, USNR

Sept. 23, 1943

I could get along with my French pretty good but Italian slays me.

PASSED BY NAVAL CENSORS

(Post Card Palermo, Italy)
LT. (j.g.) Charles A. McCall, USNR

Sept. 23, 1943

    This looks a lot like things back home but my! At the difference!

PASSED BY NAVAL CENSORS

(Post Card Palermo, Italy)
LT. (j.g.) Charles A. McCall, USNR

Sept. 23, 1943

Some of these places are a little the worse due to some *slight* explosions.

Lt. (jg.) Charles A. McCall, USNR.

Some of these places
are a little the worse
due to some slight
explosions.

Mrs. Clyde S. McCall

Lake Toxaway,

North Carolina

U.S.A.

Palermo - Piazza stazione Centrale e via Roma.

PASSED BY NAVAL CENSORS

(Post Card Palermo, Italy)
LT. (j.g.) Charles A. McCall, USNR

Sept. 23, 1943

Dear Mama,

This is real dead people who died hundres of years ago and there's thousands of them. I didn't sleep good for a few nights after I saw it but we had right much fun giving them nicknames and talking at them.

Love
Chas.

V - MAIL

PASSED BY NAVAL CENSORS

U.S.S. LCI (L) No. 42

Sept. 26, 1943

Dear Mama,

Haven't heard from you for some time but haven't had an opportunity to get any mail. Hope everyone is well.

Guess the kids have started to school by now and Daddy has started teaching leaving you and Joe Ben all alone. Where are the kids going and how is Dan making out?

Don't see much possibility of getting home this winter but one can never tell, you know. Sure would like to be there now for the squirrel season.

All's well with me and I'm doing fine.

Love to all,
Charles

POMPEI postcard book
Date unknown

Some rainy day I'll tell you all about what I saw here.*

Love,
Charles

*I wonder if he ever did. I'd love to have him here to tell us some rainy day.

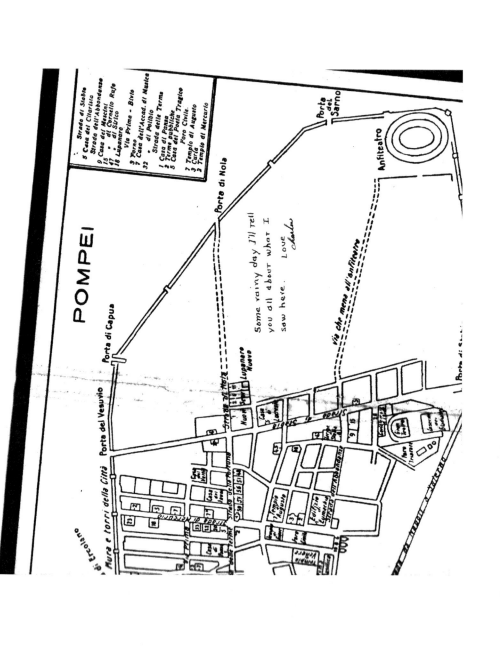

CAPRI - PANORAMA E VESUVIO.

Extending Time Of Shoe Stamps Will Prevent Last Minute Rush To Stores And Shoes Will Have To Last Longer

Sees Lots Of Action

LT. (JG.) CHARLES ALLEN McCALL, son of Mr. and Mrs. Clyde S. McCall, of Lake Toxaway, took part in the North Africa and Sicilian campaigns. He is a graduate of Rosman high school, Western Carolina Teachers college and finished at Annapolis in May, 1942. He then took four months training in diesel electrical engineering before going to sea.

DR. DUDLEY IS

Board Urges Public To Buy Better Shoes. New Stamp To Be Good November 1

The removal of the expiration date of currently valid shoe ration stamp number 18, plus the validation of airplane stamp number 1 in ration book three for one pair of shoes beginning November 1, has eliminated the possibility of a repitition of last June's "stampede" in Brevard and throughout the nation, it was pointed out here this week.

This action on the part of the OPA was anounced a few days ago.

It means, too, that every person will have to get along with two pairs of shoes a year, and many contend that will be difficult. It is explained, however, that in case of severe hardships the regulations provide that such persons can obtain special stamps from the rationing board office here.

In this connection, though, Dr. Zachary, chairman of the board, announced this week that because of the leather shortage it will be necessary for the board to be more rigid in the future that it has been in the past in the issuance of special stamps.

There is no getting around the fact that there is a shortage of leather and that we will have to do our part in the conservation program," he stated.

"Of course we are going to do all we can to take care of all hard-

CHAPTER NINE

Naples and Christmas in Italy

The landing of our forces on the beaches of Salerno marked the first Allied invasion of the Italian mainland. Because of the Italian army's failures, most notably in Sicily, Mussolini was ousted and arrested in late July of 1943. In early September the Italian forces surrendered to the Allies. However, the Germans promptly rescued Mussolini, seized control and fiercely defended the Axis stand in Italy. The establishment of a beachhead at Salerno was a hard fight lasting over ten days, but the Allies prevailed. By October 4, 1943, our troops had succeeded in taking Naples, one of the main objectives of the Salerno landings. The establishment of a base at Naples gave the Allies a launching pad for the next invasion on the Italian coast, somewhere to the north towards Rome.

Grandpa Charlie spent the last quarter of 1943 in Italy close to Naples. As those fall days passed, anticipation of the next Allied invasion increasingly mounted. Amidst the height of all this speculation came Christmas. Christmas in Italy, a dream come true under other circumstances, something to make the best of under these. The letters in this chapter paint the picture.

Candler N C
Oct 8th 1943

Dear Mrs McCall:

    I am writing you to find out if you have heard from Charlie lately. It has been over a month since we have heard from Tom, he told me in his last letter that he and Charlie was not very far apart but did not see each other for when one was in port the other was out. I am so anxious about Tom. I have a son in the hospital in the Southwest Pacific, but he is getting along fine, he happened to be sent to a hospital where his other two brothers are stationed so they see him every day. So that leaves Tom by hisself but he and Charlie have been so close to each other for a long time I hope you have heard from him. Let me know. I hope the boy of yours Tom told me about being so sick is fine now.

Sincerely,

Mrs C.A. Mallonee
Candler N.C.

PASSED BY NAVAL CENSORS

U.S.S. LCI (L) No. 42

October 8, 1943

Dear Mama,

I haven't been able to write to you for several days and I guess you have been worrying about me quite a bit. Everything is fine and I couldn't be better. In circumstances like these it is not only impossible for me to send mail but it is also very seldom that I get any. I made a good long trip by plane the other day, however and picked up some mail for the ship and there were three letters from you. It sure was good to hear after so long and to know that everyone is well.

You said that school had started and that everyone was gone but you and Joe Ben. Guess it's rather lonely. Is Dan going to Rosman too? Let me know how the kids make out.

I had a letter from Helen and they all seem to be well enough. She hadn't heard from you for sometime. It is hard to believe that Suzanne is talking and running around. Guess I have been gone longer than it seems. It will soon be a year now since I was home last, and there seems to be little possibility that I will be back soon.

I also had letters from Pettit, Essie Reid, Mr. Deans and several other friends—eighteen of them in all and it sure made me happy. You asked if I heard from Pettit often—yes and no. I heard from her very regularly for a while and then there was some mix-up and I didn't hear from her or she from me for a good long while. It seems to be straightened out now, however, and I have had several letters from her lately. She has been pretty good about writing and in my opinion she is a pretty well gal. The last letter I had from her she was either being transferred to Asheville or resigning her job. She has been in Washington now for almost a year and has been pretty lonesome and homesick the whole time. That is a pretty tough place for a girl to live these days and I don't blame her a bit for getting out of it—in fact, I encouraged it.

I have received only one box of the candy you have mailed but I guess the other boxes are on the way and I will probably get them soon. Helen has also mailed me a box. The papers haven't started coming yet. I am anxious to get some of them.

I think I saw a fellow from Brevard that I know in Sicily some time ago by the name of Harry Johnson (son of the chairman of the Board of Elections) but I didn't have a chance to confirm my belief. Outside of that, I have seen no one from around there.

Everything is well so don't worry about me.

Love Always,
Charles

V - Mail

PASSED BY NAVAL CENSORS

U.S.S. LCI (L) No.42

October 12, 1943

Dear Mama,

I have time for just a few lines to let you know that all is well. I have been pretty busy for the past few days but hope to have a little more time soon so that I can catch up with my correspondence.

I haven't heard from John for months and am wondering just what has happened to him. I am anxious to keep in close contact with him from here on in because there is a possibility that he will be assigned to this theater and if he is I should like very much to know about it.

There has been no mail recently so there isn't much to write about. Have been having plenty of *fun*.

Love,
Charles

PASSED BY NAVAL CENSORS

U.S.S. LCI (L) No.42

October 23, 1943

Dear Mama,

We got mail yesterday for the first time in several weeks and I really did O.K. I got six boxes of candy, a carton of cigarettes, seven newspapers and something over thirty letters. Three of the boxes of candy and the cigarettes were from you—thanks a million—I sure have been filling up on candy and it really is good. Six "Transylvania Times" and one "Citizen" came and I enjoyed them no end. There were several letters from you the latest one of which, I believe, was dated September 29.

I am very upset over Dan's condition and suggest that you have him thoroughly examined immediately. I would place very little faith in what the "County Nurse" has to say but even a suggestion of something serious should be looked into at once. This business of him tiring quickly makes me wonder if something isn't still wrong with his lungs. Have Dr. Wilkerson examine him thoroughly and let me know what he suggests. I see no reason, however, for taking him out of school but perhaps I don't understand the circumstances.

I found the papers very interesting and had no end of fun out of the one which told of the feud between the McCalls and the Daves. Brooks*, our executive officer, is a Jew from Cincannati—very serious minded and communistically inclined. He and I were sitting quietly reading our mail last night and after I had finished the story I looked up causally and said, "Well it won't be long until winter, I see here where the folks down home are feudin' again". "They are!" he says, excited as heck. "Yeah", I said, "They got one of my uncles the first go around". He swallowed it hook, line and sinker as he usually does my tall tales and has spread the news throughout the whole Flotilla. I was also interested to learn that so many fellows from there are in this theatre—can't understand why I haven't seen some of them. Will you try to get Harold McNeely's address and send it to me

Am enclosing a little Christmas present for all of you to be used as you see fit. Wish I could send more but find it impossible at the present. I have allotted most of my salary to a savings account and as a result my pay checks are rather slim. I think I am doing pretty good, however, since I'm saving $125 a month not counting what I have been putting in war bonds. By the way, in case I get bumped off, my account is with Wachovia Bank and Trust in Asheville.

Everything is fine with me but don't expect me home soon. Have a good Christmas and don't hold off a bit because of me because I'm going to have a good one too. Look up my gal if you have a chance—would like for you to see her (am sending Ma Pettit money for her present). Write often and keep your chin up—we're winning the war.

Love to all
Charles A Moley

* **Ens. L. J. Brooks.** Found on Lt. McCall's faded carbon copy of "Home Directory of Officers of LCI(L) Flotilla One, dated November 26, 1943, and found amongst the letters. Grandpa Charlie called him "Brooks" and "Brooksie", but his first name was Len. You will see all three of these names in future letters. So far, sadly, I have been unsuccessful in finding him or his family.

Grandpa Charlie is on the left, and I am reasonably certain that Brooks is on the right with their crew surrounding them.

V - Mail

PASSED BY NAVAL CENSORS

U.S.S. LCI (L) No.42

October 29, 1943

Dear Mama,

I think I forgot to tell you that the package of V-mail you sent reached me. Thank you very much—I needed it.

I'm well and getting along fine. Sure am going to miss being home for Christmas this year. Hope you folks have a good one.

I haven't heard from John for months and wonder where he is. Has he been home yet. I would like to have a picture of him in Uniform.

Ducky's letter came the other day—will answer it soon.

Love to all
Charles

V - Mail

PASSED BY NAVAL CENSORS

U.S.S. LCI (L) No.42

11-1-43

Dear Mama,

Here it is the first of November and I'm still not home. Well, there is one consolation—I'm not disappointed because I didn't expect it. Some of the officers are being sent back now but I can't see my number coming up any time soon. It sure would be fine to get back for a little while but I'm sure that after a few weeks there, I would long to be back where things are happening so I may as well be satisfied where I am.

I have seen quite a bit of Tom* the last few days and we have had a lot of fun exchanging news etc. We had dates with some Army nurses last night and sure had a good time. One of the Nurses was from Greenville, South Carolina and it was almost like getting home again for a while.

A very interesting thing happened to me a couple of days ago. The gangway watch came in and told me that there was a man outside who thought that he was a relative of mine. I couldn't imagine who on earth it might be and naturally was quite excited. It turned out to be Marcus McCall from Greenville. He is a brother to Bob, you know, the one who is at the Naval Academy. I write to Bob and he had written to Marcus giving him the number of my ship. He had seen the ship several times but had not had a chance to come aboard. It had been so long since I had seen him that I didn't know him, of course, but we had a lot of fun renewing acquaintances and exchanging news. I went over to his ship yesterday and gave him a box of my candy and had another long talk. It sure was quite a treat.

You asked me about the weather over here. I can't tell you much about it but it isn't nearly as cold as it would be there this time of year. Guess you will be getting some snow pretty soon and I sure would like to see some of it.

The mail isn't coming through so good now but I get a letter now and then. I had a letter from Helen yesterday and they seem to be getting along fine. She says that Roy is buying an automobile so I suppose that makes him happy. I can't wait to see that kid of theirs. I am wondering what has happened to John—I haven't heard from him in months and you haven't mentioned anything about him recently. Has he been home? If he hasn't and when he does, have him send me a picture of himself.

Hope this finds all you well and fine. I'm O.K. Write often.

Love,
Charles

* Grandpa Charlie is referring to Lt. Thomas L. Mallonee from Candler, N.C. Tom was one of his best friends and is mentioned often throughout this correspondence. You will notice there are two letters in the book from Tom's mother, Mrs. Mallonee, to Grandma Delphie.

V - Mail

PASSED BY NAVAL CENSORS

U.S.S. LCI (L) No.42

November 7, 1943

Dear Mama,

Haven't heard from you recently but will drop you just a few lines to let you know that everything is O.K. The mail isn't coming through so well at present but I expect to be getting some before long.

Subject matter for letters gets scarcer and scarcer as time goes by, it seems. I have been away from home so long now that there are few contacts left to write about and everything here is censored.

You asked me something about a number in your last letter and I suppose you were referring to a service number which officers don't use. I had a service number at the Naval Academy but I don't believe it is used any more. It was 406-44-59. My file no. is 119509.

Space is gone so will close.

Love to all
Charles

V - Mail

PASSED BY NAVAL CENSORS

U.S.S. LCI (L) No.42

Nov. 11, 1943

Dear Mama,

It's Armistice day and a beautiful Fall day at that. Even though it is rather premature, I have been thinking about what it will be like when the next Armistice comes. No doubt it will be a great day back there with a lot of gaity, etc. but I believe It would be a greater thrill to be right here in the thick of it when the news comes in. It's hard to imagine what it will be like in any case.

Your letter of October 19 came yesterday. It was the first one for several days and I was glad to hear from you. I'll bet Ducky really does enjoy her music lessons. I often wish I had taken them.

Everything is fine with me.

Love to all
Charles

PASSED BY NAVAL CENSORS

Buon Natale
Italian Postcard

Nov. 14, 1943

Lt. (j.g.) Charles A. McCall, USNR

Season's greetings

and love always to

you both.

Your
Son

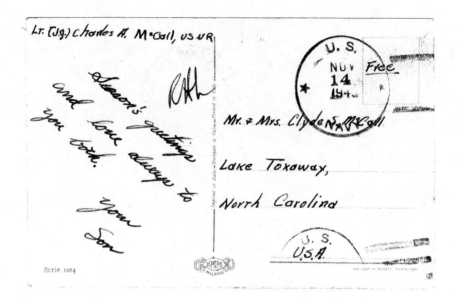

Lt. (j.g.) Charles A. McCall, US NR

R.H.

Season's greetings
and love always to
you both.

Your
Son

Scrie 1014

Mr. & Mrs. Clyde N. McCall

Lake Toxaway,

North Carolina

Buon Natale

November 19, 1943

Dear Folks,

There is nothing I enjoy more than a good long letter now and then and in order to get them, I suppose I should write one now an then. It is rather a difficult task under the present circumstances but I will see what I can do. I wonder, however, if it is advisable at the present time since V-mail is about the only type that is coming through to me. They say that all regular and second class mail is being held up because of Christmas packages and there must be something to it because I have had nothing but V-mail letters for almost a month now.

One exception was this afternoon when I received two packages—a box of candy from Helen and the cake and candy from you. Thanks a lot for the nice box—it's all very good. The cake had hardened quite a bit in transit but was (and is, because I am eating a piece of it as I write this letter) very delicious in spite of that.

I have received no Newspapers for several weeks.

I have been eating like a King for the past few days. A ship loaded with fresh food came in and I saw to it that we got our part. A few of the things we got were beef (steak, roast & stew), a mutton, pork, pork sausage, fresh oysters, hamburger, butter, eggs, cheese, cabbage, carrots, onions, apples, oranges, turnips, hams, etc. So you see I have been faring fine. The things that I enjoyed most were the eggs, butter and onions. We usually have only powdered eggs and since they aren't very good in the first place you soon get awfully tired of them. We have canned butter which isn't too bad but it is very thick (vegetable compound and not oleo) and tends to stick to the roof of your mouth while you are eating it. The fresh butter was wonderful. And the onions—umm! I have been eating two at meals times and three of four between meals. Our mess boy, a young negro, can't understand what I do with all of them—it keeps him busy peeling them for me. At times like this, as far as food is concerned, we probably fare much better than most of the people back home, I guess.

There are lots of Army hospitals around here and since an English speaking girl is of more value that rubies, most of my spare evenings are spent with a nurse. I might pause here to say that they are doing a wonderful job over here and in a lot of instances have shown more "guts" than a lot of men would show. They are all very kind and friendly and serve as an excellent morale builder for the men. To go on with my tale, one that I was with a few nights ago told me that there were two McCall sisters in her outfit. I was immediately interested and more so when she told me they were from South Carolina. She invited me up the next afternoon to meet them and I went. Their names were Julia and Olivia and they are from Anderson, S.C. I don't recall their father's name but we were unable to trace any relationship—for which I am not too sorry because the younger one, Julia, is very charming and we get along nicely; she was down to the ship and had supper with me tonight. Their father came from Georgia so I don't suppose there is any relationship, do you? While we're on the subject, I saw Markus again today. He is seeing plenty of action but doing fine.

As far as the war is concerned, there is very little I can say except that from where I sit, it looks pretty darned good. No doubt, the hardest fighting is yet to come but we're ready and, at this stage of the game, are more blood thirsty than Hitler's goose-stepping stooges ever were at their height. Just let us at them! As you have read, the boys on the Italian front are having a tough time—and I mean *tough*, but they are doing O.K. and will continue to do so because we're headed for Berlin and the only command we will know until the day we arrive is "*Forward*".

I would like for you to secure a copy of the Sept 27 issue of "Newsweek" magazine and ready the article by Al Newman on the Salerno invasion. Am enclosing a copy of a message we all received from Gen. Eisenhower, the last paragraph of which is very expressive of my personal feelings and those of all the fellows over here. This war is being fought by a group of very serious minded young men. The mass hysteria and high degree of emotionalism characteristic of past wars is ^very^ noticeably lacking in this one and I think it is a wonderful thing. We know our aims, we have considered the cost, and with cool heads and determined wills we're here to win and we *shan't be stopped.*

Guess I've almost overdone myself in writing this much. It is impossible to convey to you the type of life I live and the thoughts I have but a few rambling words like these may help a little. I'm happy, healthy, and enjoying life—that's enough, isn't it? So don't worry about me.

Love to all
Charles

P.S. Daddy's letter received, will answer soon.

C.

A
Personal Message

from

General DWIGHT D. EISENHOWER

November 8, 1943

ALLIED FORCE HEADQUARTERS
Office of the Commander-in-Chief

To:

Admiral Sir John J. D. Cunningham, K.C.B., C.V.O.

General Sir Harold R. L. G. Alexander, G.C.B., C.S.I., D.S.O., M.C.

Air Chief Marshal Sir Arthur W. Tedder. G.C.B.

As the Commander of American Forces in this theater I am sending, on the anniversary of the initial landings in North Africa, a written message to every American soldier, sailor and airman. Since this message includes mention of purposes and aspirations in this war, it is scarcely appropriate for it to be addressed directly to any but my own countrymen. Yet British and American Forces of all services have here so closely and effectively associated themselves together in a common cause that I feel impelled, whenever there is occasion for reviewing accomplishments of American Forces, to assure you and all those under your respective commands that my thanks and my pride as Allied Commander-in-Chief, go out to them in equal measure. Consequently, if you deem it proper, I will be grateful if a copy of this message could be sent also to each member of all British Forces in the theater. I know that your officers and all other ranks wi'l clearly understand my hope that they will merely substitute the name of their own country wherever mine is mentioned, and accept my best wishes and gratitude for their splendid services, in the spirit they are meant.

Very sincerely,

Dwight D Eisenhower

a

AMERICAN HEADQUARTERS IN NORTH AFRICA
Office of the Commander-in-Chief

Personal from General Eisenhower to all men and women of the American Military and Civil Forces in the North African Theater:

We have reached the first anniversary of initial British-American landings in this theater.

You came here to take part in a crusade to eliminate ruthless aggression from the earth and to guarantee to yourselves and to your children security against the threat of domination by arrogant despotism.

During the year just past, you have written a memorable chapter in the history of American arms, a chapter in which are recorded deeds of valor, of sacrifice, of endurance and of unswerving loyalty. You have worked effectively and in friendly cooperation with the Armies, Navies and Air Forces of our Allies and have established in a foreign land a reputation for decency and dignity in conduct. Hour by hour your efforts are contributing toward the ultimate defeat of mighty military machines that hoped to conquer the world. You are just as surely the protectors and supporters of American democracy as your forefathers were its founders.

From my heart I thank each of you for the services you have so well performed, in the air, on the sea, in the front lines and in our ports and bases.

All of us salute with reverence the memory of the comrades we have lost, as we earnestly pray that Almighty God will bring comfort to their loved ones.

But we must now look forward, because for us there can be no thought of turning back until our task has been fully accomplished.

We are on the mainland of Europe, carrying the battle, daily, closer to the vitals of the enemy. More Americans and more of our Allies will continue to follow steadily into the fight. All of us will work together as one. With the gallant and powerful Russian Army pounding the European enemy on the East and with growing forces seeking out and penetrating weak spots in his defenses from all other directions, his utter defeat—even if not yet definitely in sight—is certain. Victory will likewise be ours in the far off Pacific, where Allied Forces are already on the offensive and where unconquerable China, awaiting the time when the full power of the Allies may come to her assistance, continues to defy one of the most powerful and vicious of our enemies.

The heart of America supports our every endeavour. Reports of sporadic troubles on the home front are occasioned by the ill-considered actions of a relatively few individuals. Let us always remember that our great nation of 130,000,000 people is ceaselessly working and sacrificing to provide us weapons, equipment and supplies, and to send us an increasing flow of reinforcements. Our Allies march forward with us. The God of Justice fights on our side.

Let us, then, strengthen ourselves for the tasks yet lying ahead. With high courage let us redouble our efforts and multiply the fury of our blows so that we may the more quickly re-cross the seas to our own homeland with the glorious word that the last enemy stronghold has fallen and with the proud knowledge of having done, in our time, our duty to our beloved country.

V - Mail

PASSED BY NAVAL CENSORS

U.S.S. LCI (L) No.42

11-20-43

Dear Mama,

I wrote a long letter yesterday but I sent it regular mail and it will probably be some time in coming through—so will drop a few lines on this.

I had a letter from you this morning and a Transylvania Times—the one with my picture in it. Glad everyone is well—I'm fine.

It's quite a bit colder here than it has been but if I stay here I don't expect as cold a winter as you will have. Isn't it rather unusual for snow to fall even in Highlands during October?

I mailed a bunch of Italian Christmas cards several days ago hope you get yours. I also mailed some other cards to Ducky.

That's all for now.

Love,
Charles

PASSED BY NAVAL CENSORS

U.S.S. LCI (L) No.42

November 30, 1943

Dear Mama,

The mail came yesterday and I got a sack full. There was about a dozen from you all of which I enjoyed very much. Several of your V-mails had been sent to wrong addresses due to the faintness of the address. Do you use a pencil for them? Pencil photographs very poorly and makes them rather hard to read. Also had letters from Dan and Jerry which I plan to answer right away. Letters from Pettit, Ma Pettit, Mrs. Wilkerson and various others.

I must tell you about my Thanksgiving dinner—it was wonderful. We had turkey and dressing, potatoes and gravy, peas, cranberries, pumpkin pie, ice cream, fruit cake and coffee. I really filled up.

Sure would liked to have seen John. I had a letter from him written Sept. 28.

This is just between us. I've never been so mad in my life—I'm boiling over and have to tell someone to get it off my mind. Pettit told me about it in a letter received today. Junior Curry* was home, you know, and for the first few days he was there he was out with Pettit a lot. He took her to Cullowhee to homecoming and introduced her to every girl I have ever dated there. He took her to Irene Hamilton's home and they discussed me for hours (Curry was once very much in love with Irene and I "cut his water off"). Then he has the audacity to take Pettit out the next night and propose to her! Of course, Pettit told him where to go *right away* but it makes me so mad I could shoot him easily. I guess he was trying to "get even" but I think his methods were very underhanded and I intend to tell him so.

I received another "Transylvania Times" yesterday but my "Citizen" doesn't seem to be coming through very well. The candy comes O.K., I've had several boxes recently. You can kind of ease up a bit on it if you like—I have more than I can eat.

Pettit has gone to Georgia to work and live with her Dad. I see Tom rather often recently. I got the clippings you sent. Tom is worried sick over his brother—he can't hear from home.

Guess that's all for this time. Give everyone my love.

Yours,
Charles

* After Grandpa Charlie died, Grandma Alice married this guy. Yes, the infamous, Jim Curry! The truth really is stranger than fiction!

PASSED BY NAVAL CENSORS

U.S.S. LCI (L) No.42

December 1, 1943

Dear Mama,

I wrote you yesterday but I received some pictures I had made since then and thought you might like one. They are pretty cheap excuses but the best I can do under the circumstances—in fact I was lucky to get any at all.

Tom and I were ashore last night with a couple of Nurses (The McCalls) and had a very enjoyable time. I haven't been able to get ashore very often for liberty recently and it's good to have a little diversion, and with only a few hundred American girls for over a million men you're pretty lucky to rate one.

I'm fine as a fiddle, don't worry about me.

Love,
Charles

PASSED BY NAVAL CENSORS

U.S.S. LCI (L) No.42

Dr. & Mrs. J.B. Wilkerson
Brevard,
North Carolina

December 4, 1943

Dear Mrs. Wilkerson,

Your very nice letter came yesterday and was thoroughly enjoyed. It was very sweet of you to remember me and you would find it hard to realize how much your kind words of encouragement mean to me out here in "The land that time forgot."

Glad to hear that you are all getting along so well and your news of my family was greatly appreciated. Mama often mentions you in her letters and is always delighted by your visits. And I quite agree with you in your opinion of her—I think she's just about the swellest Mom in the world. I have been left nothing to desire when it comes to parents. Guess we all feel that way, don't we?

John hadn't been home at the time you were writing but since then Mama says he was there for a few days. Did you see him? I haven't seen him since he entered the army and would give my right arm for some time with him now. Perhaps it won't be too long.

Woman, you're driving me crazy! Fried chicken, biscuits, pound cake! Yum, Yum! Just wait until I get back and you'll regret your bargain—I'll eat you out of house and home. It breaks my heart to say so but I wouldn't advise you to mail the cake—packages are sometimes months enroute. Just wait, I'll make up for it.

You can do me a favor, however, if it isn't asking too much. Brevard College is to get (or probably already has) a new professor by the name of Dr. (Ph.D.) Bramlett. He was formerly at Cullowhee and a very good friend of mine. So if, during one of your spare moments (if you have such) you will drop down to see him and welcome him to our beloved county ^for me^ I should greatly appreciate it. He is rather old, comes from a Haywood county farm and is as "homey" as an old hat but very brilliant and an authority on current events. I think you will enjoy meeting him.

I should like to tell you all about myself, where I have been, what I have seen, etc. but I'm afraid that will have to wait. The historical sights I have seen such as the ruins of famous Roman cities, catacombs, cathedrals, volcanos, casbas, etc. have been a liberal education within themselves. I shall never regret my time spent in the Navy.

Wish I could make my letter as long and as interesting as yours but any attempt at that would be vein. So I'll sign off sending my best regards to you all. Remember me to Bert and the Doc. Let me hear from you again.

> Yours for Victory
> Charles

V - Mail

PASSED BY NAVAL CENSORS

U.S.S. LCI (L) No.42

December 10, 1943

Dear Mama,

Haven't had a chance to write for a few days so will drop just a line to let you know that everything is O.K. Hope you folks are all fine.

I haven't received any mail for several days now but expect to get it soon. And when I do, I'm expecting several Christmas boxes. Your fruit cake is due and so is one from Helen. Petit has mailed me two boxes which should be here and Miss Camp from Cullowhee, whom I correspond with regularly has mailed a box. Several others say they have mailed something so if it all comes through I should have a very Merry Christmas.

May your holiday season be joyous and may the New Year bring us all what we desire most—Victory.

Love to all,
Charles

PASSED BY NAVAL CENSORS

U.S.S. LCI (L) No.42

Jerry and Dan McCall
Lake Toxaway,
North Carolina

December 12, 1943

Dear Boys,

What kind of an army is this that you guys belong to anyway? First I hear from you as General Jerry and Private Dan and then only a few weeks later it's General Dan and Private Jerry. What did you do Dan, give Jerry a general court martial? And then how did you advance so rapidly? What ever you did, I'm very anxious to hear about it—perhaps I could use your methods and become an Admiral within a few days.

Your letters were good and I enjoyed them very much. I believe, however, that you could make them just a little longer next time, couldn't you. You can tell me all about school, what you are studying, what you do during recess periods, etc. You can also tell me about your Christmas holidays, the presents you got and whether it snowed or not. Did you get the Italian Christmas cards I sent you? Dan, you must be learning very fast to be able to write such a good letter—guess you'll be writing books pretty soon, won't you? And Jerry will be designing a new type of battleship.

It has been a year now since I saw you boys and I'll bet you have really grown up. How much do you weigh now? By the time I get back you will both be so big that I will be afraid to play around with you much.

How is Joe Ben? I guess he gets rather lonesome while both of you are away at school, doesn't he?

I can't tell you very much about myself except that I am getting along fine. I keep pretty busy most of the time and for that reason have not answered your letters sooner. I have seen a lot of interesting things recently which I will have to tell you about some time. Of all the things I have seen, I think the one that gave me the greatest thrill was an active volcano. It is some sight to see fire and smoke boiling out of the inside of the earth.

I am enclosing two of three pieces of Italian money for you. They are five and ten lire (pronounced Lir—a, "i" as in lit) notes. The present exchange value of the lira is once cent so the notes are worth a nickle and a dime. Italy has a wide variety of coins and I have a good collection of them but am not permitted to mail any to you but will bring them when I come home. I also have a lot of English and French coins for you and by the time I get back am hoping to add to them some of the German variety.

Let me hear from you soon and take care of things at home. Give my love to Ducky and all the rest.

Your little brother
Charles

V - Mail

PASSED BY NAVAL CENSORS

U.S.S. LCI (L) No.42

December 13, 1943

Dear Mama,

Your V-mail of November 18 came yesterday. Glad to hear that everyone is O.K. I'm fine.

It seems that the money I sent arrived sooner than I expected it to. I'm glad you could use to to an advantage but it was really meant for Christmas. I wanted you to get everyone presents for me since I will be unable to do so myself.

As soon as you get it I would like for you to send me John's address. He doesn't seem to be very prompt about writing to me and I would like to drop him a line.

Sure hope it will be possible for Helen and Roy to get there for Christmas. I hear from her rather often but I'm afraid I don't write her as often as I should.

Everything's O.K. Here

Love,
Charles

PASSED BY NAVAL CENSORS

U.S.S. LCI (L) No.42

December 17, 1943

Dear Mama,

Had a couple of letters from you today and the one from Joe Ben. Glad to hear that everyone is well. Everything is fine with me.

The picture of John was in one of the letters and I certainly was glad to get it. It was rather hard for me to imagine him in a uniform not having seen him in one but I must say that he wears it like a man. The captain's comment when he saw it was "He's better looking than you are, isn't he" and I'm inclined to agree with him. However, don't tell him I said so.

Had a letter from Pettit today telling me about meeting you folks. She said that she thought Daddy was rather surprised at her size—and that surprises me. I should think that Daddy knew me well enough to know how I like my women. Tell Joe Ben that he has beaten my time and I'm jealous—Pettit fell in love with him immediately.

Haven't received any Christmas boxes yet but hope they will arrive soon. Neither have I had any newspapers for some time.

Everything is swell here—expect to be home before many more months go by.

Love to all
Charlie

December 22, 1944
(actually 1943)

Dear Mama,

Because of the news today I thought you would be interested in hearing from me. I'm rather worn out but undamaged. I haven't had any sleep for a couple of days but am all ready now for a good hot bath and a night's rest, I hope.

The last picture of John you sent me is very good, I think. I think he has become a man since I saw him last. It sure would be wonderful to see him again for a while.

I have a suggestion for you for the next time you want to send me something—a carton of "Spud" cigarettes "cools will do if you can't find the "Spuds." There are times when I smoke entirely too much and a mentholated cigarette is just what I need—we can't get them here.

I did something a few days ago that may have been a mistake but I'm not worried. There are times when Pettit don't write very often and I don't like it. This time I had gone almost a month without a letter from her so I wrote her and told her to "go fly her kite." Think I know how it will turn out but just wanted her to know I don't give a darn.

Hope everyone there is well.

Love to all
Charles

December 22, 1944

Dear Mama,

Because of the news today I thought you would be interested in hearing from me. I'm rather worn out but undamaged. I haven't had any sleep ~~for~~ for a couple of days but am all ready now for a good hot bath and a nights' rest, I hope.

The last picture of John you sent me is very good, I think. I think he has become a man since I saw him last. It sure would be wonderful to see him again for a while.

I have a suggestion for you for the next time you want to send me something — a carton of "Spud" cigarettes "cools will do if you can't find

PASSED BY NAVAL CENSORS

U.S.S. LCI (L) No.42

UNITED STATES NAVY

December 26, 1943

Dear Folks,

Hope you had an enjoyable Christmas. Mine was fine.

Christmas Eve Night the captain and I had dates with some nurses. We went to their tent, poped corn on their stove and then opened all their Christmas presents. It was a whole lot like Christmas. We went to church then at eleven o'clock (night) and came back to the ship and opened our own boxes. Your fruit cake* came but the other box hasn't. Thanks a lot it was delicious. I went to church again at ten o'clock on Christmas morning and came back to a really good Christmas dinner. We had turkey, dressing, cranberry sauce, fresh peas and potatoes, apple pie, cake, coffee and nuts. Tom and I spent the afternoon together.

Received Daddy's letter and will answer it tonight. Too bad about Jerry's nose—he'll have to be a little more careful.

Did Helen & Roy get home for Christmas? I haven't heard from them for some time.

I have to go so will close for how.

Love,
Charles

*See, Casi & Erin, I told you this used to be a Christmas treat. You girls must not have inherited the fruit cake gene! Sorry it made you sick!

Madama Butterfly

Tragedia in 3 atti. Libretto di Illica e G. Giacosa

Musica di Giacomo Puccini

Madama Butterfly	Susy Moretti
Suzuki	Bice Citarelli
Kate Pinkerton	Lina Mazzei
B. F. Pinkerton . . .	
Console Sha...	

TEATRO DI S. CARLO

Stagione Lirica 1943-1944

SOTTO LA DIREZIONE DELL'AUTORITÀ MILITARE BRITANNICA
DI NAPOLI

Programma

PREZZO

Lire Cinque (Lire 5,00)

Price : Five Lire

CHAPTER TEN

Anzio, Rome, France and Back

Anzio, just north of Naples on the Italian coast, was chosen by the Allies for the next invasion. The strategy was to surprise the German army by landing troops on the Anzio beaches. After catching the German off guard, our soldiers would immediately advance inland toward the prize of Rome. Churchill's idea, the strategic wisdom of the Anzio landings had been debated for a month by Allied commanders prior the invasion, and is still being debated by military experts today. Significant Allied forces and Naval landing craft had been sent to England in preparation for the Normandy invasion (D-Day). There was concern among military leaders that the Allies could not be successful at Anzio with the remaining skeleton force. According to military historian Irwin J. Kappes, "It would be one of the riskiest gambles of World War II. Nevertheless, just after dawn on 21 January 1944 a motley armada of 240 ships — mostly amphibious landing craft set sail from the bay of Naples. . . . None knew exactly where they were headed, but a rehearsal for the landing had left little room for speculation. It had to be somewhere between Naples and Rome, right where German strength was concentrated." The naval operations and landing of troops was an undisputed success. By the end of the day January 22, 1944 over 35,000 soldiers and 3,500 vehicles had landed on the beaches of Anzio. However, due to faulty intelligence regarding the size of German forces in the area and the decision of the American general in command to delay the advance inland, Anzio became a deathtrap for Allied soldiers and sailors. Perched atop mountains that formed a ring around the beachhead and harbor, German troops had Allied forces surrounded. Our men and ships were sitting ducks. Again from Mr. Kappes, "In many ways, Anzio was much like the Pacific war. There was no rear area that was safe from attack. If you were at Anzio at all, you were in the front lines. No bunker, no ship, was safe. . . . For four months the invaders battled foul winter weather, heavy bombing and artillery fire to sustain the Anzio Beachhead. Through the long struggle . . . our troops were strongly supported by naval gunfire, airpower and a shuttle of ships and craft that braved air and submarine attack to deliver reinforcements. . . . In what many consider a land battle, there were a total to 17 ships lost: ten British and seven U.S. Navy. In this action, 166 American sailors were wounded and 160 made the ultimate sacrifice in the cause of freedom. . . . ' Anzio beachhead,' naval historian Samuel Elliot Morrison wrote, 'should endure in our memories as a symbol of heroic tenacity."

Your Grandpa Charlie wrote in the Military Service section of the family Bible, a gift for my sixth Christmas, "Navy Cross at Anzio for Rescue of *LCVP." I remember seeing the Cross, but in all of the shuffle after Grandma Alice's remarriage, tragically, it was lost. As you will see, he writes little about Anzio. He never talked about it except for one time years later when he asked me a question, which I now believe referred to the undisputed hell that was Anzio. I'll tell you about his question later.

Ultimately after 7,000 killed and 36,000 wounded or missing, the Allied forces captured Rome on June 5, 1944. The following day the Allies invaded northern France at Normandy. Hopefully you all have some knowledge of D-Day. If not I would suggest that you watch *Saving Private Ryan*. That movie will tell you more than I could ever write on the subject. It was right after D-Day, June 6, 1944, that Grandpa Charlie's younger brother, Carlos John McCall, went missing in action and ultimately became a German prisoner of war. He was a member of the Army Air Corp (Air Force). You will read a lot about John in this chapter. Grandpa Charlie remained in Italy with the LCI(L)-42 through the summer. He got to see Rome and other Italian landmarks. He even saw the opera *Madame Butterfly* in Naples, which must have been an intensely beautiful and emotional experience, especially considering what he had recently been through. One letter will tell a charming story about dating an Italian girl. And you will find in this chapter the beautiful Mother's Day letter of 1944.

From August 15 to September 23, 1944 the LCI(L)-42 participated in the invasion of Southern France. Paris was liberated on August 25 (your birthday, Casi). Grandpa Charlie writes of the beauty of Southern France, both the countryside and the women! When Uncle Hal and I were in St. Tropez for our 25th wedding anniversary and walked the surrounding beaches, I had the strangest feeling that my Father had been there. Turns out I was right!

By mid-December 1944, after almost two years, Lt. Charles Allen McCall was back where he shipped off to war, Little Creek, Virginia. The war was not over and he had orders to a new ship. The only other thing Grandpa Charlie knew for sure was that he wanted to get married. The story continues.

*Landing Craft, Vehicle, Personnel

V - MAIL
(Passed by Naval Sensors)

U.S.S. LCI (L) No. 42
January 16, 1943 (1944)

Dear Mama,

The mail came a couple of days ago and I had several letters from you plus two swell boxes of candy. The candy was the best I have had yet and I sure did enjoy it—thanks a million. I also received several papers—both kinds.

I wonder if you will do a little shopping for me. First determine whether or not you can insure a package to me and if you can shop around for me a good wristwatch. I am willing to pay as much as $75 if I can get a *good* Elgin, Waltham or Hamilton. If you can find one, let me know and I will send you the money.

Everything is fine with me. We're working hard and I haven't been able to write much and probably won't be for some time. Hope everyone there is well!

Love,
Charles

V - MAIL
(Passed by Naval Sensors)

U.S.S. LCI (L) No. 42
Jan. 20, 1943 (1944)

Dear Mama,

The mail came today for the first time in several days and I had three letters from you and a nice big box of candy. Thanks a lot for the candy, I'm saving it for a special occasion. The most recent letter was a V-mail of Jan. 3 which is much later than usual. Glad to hear that everyone is well. I'm doing fine.

You asked about the bank statements—you needn't forward them. The only thing I am interested in is to know that my allotment goes through, and I have been receiving the deposit slips. I don't know why they send the deposit slips here & the statements to my home address.

Best regards to everyone.

Love,
Charles

V - MAIL
(Passed by Naval Sensors)

U.S.S. LCI (L) No. 42
1/27/43 (1944)

Dear Folks,

Just a few lines to let you know that everything is O.K. We haven't had mail since I wrote you last so there isn't much to say.

We celebrated our first anniversary on the ship yesterday. It's been an eventful year and I hope our luck will continue as well as it has so far.

Have you heard from John recently? As soon as he is assigned a permanent address I would like for you to send it to me. I haven't heard from him recently.

About Bert's ring—the reason I haven't sent is because I can't insure it from here and I was afraid to take the risk. I am mailing now, however, and hope it makes the trip O.K.

Love to all
Charles

(Passed by Naval Sensors)

UNITED STATES NAVY

February 1, 1944

Dear Mama,

Had several letters from you a couple of days ago. Glad to hear that everyone is O.K. I'm getting along fine. Jerry's and Ducky's letters came. Tell them I will answer as soon as I can. And tell Ducky that I'm afraid there will be no more post cards. A new censorship rule which became effective a few days ago prohibits our mailing them. If she would like, however, I will continue collecting them for her and bring them when I come home.

We got a big load of fresh food yesterday which has boosted my morale a hundred percent. We were getting pretty low and the meals weren't very appetizing, but now we're fixed. We very seldom run short.

When you send another box to me I wonder if you will try to include a couple of cases of Schick injector razor blades. I have been out of them for some time and have been having to use my electric razor which I don't like. You may find it hard to locate Schick blades since they're rather scarce, it seems. And I also need a small calendar—the smaller the better if you happen to run across one.

I had my first cold of the season a couple of days ago but I about have it whipped now. My health has been pretty good since I've been over here for which I am thankful.

It's hard to imagine Tom and Ick big enough to join the Navy. It's a good place for them if they can take it.

Guess that's all for now.

Love to all
Charlie

V - MAIL
(Passed by Naval Sensors)

U.S.S. LCI (L) No. 42
2/6/44

Dear Mama,

I haven't had any mail since I wrote last but expect some within a few days. Hope all of you are well, I'm fine.

In a short while I will have in a year of continuous foreign sea duty. The Navy has a policy of sending personell back to the U.S. for a rehabilitation period after eighteen months of hazardous duty, *where practical.* So I guess I have something to look forward to but I have very little faith in the prospects. The war over here might be over by that time, anyway, so why worry. I would, however, like to go home for a few days between this and the Pacific.

Spring will soon be here and I'll welcome it. Guess you'll be getting a garden ready soon. Write often

Charles

(Passed by Naval Sensors)

U.S.S. LCI (L) No. 42

Sunday Afternoon
February 20, 1944

Dear Mama,

The mail finally came through a couple of days ago and I really got a pile. There were five letters from you and it sure was good to hear from you again. Glad everyone is O.K. I'm fine but a little sleepy this afternoon—think I'll get a nap as soon as I finish this.

I had a very interesting experience this morning. There was no protestant services near here so I went to Catholic services (Mass) with a Catholic friend of mine. It was a native Cathedral, very beautiful, and I didn't understand the language but that didn't make so much difference since the Catholic mass is almost all said in Latin anyway. It was very interesting and very beautiful but I don't understand their method of worship.

I was glad to hear that Doris has gone to be with John for a while. He should enjoy himself as much as possible now because a little later it's going to be harder. Hope they can get a good place to stay.

When I say Jim Galloway he gave me Lucy's address and I wrote her. I had a nice long reply in the last mail. She and the folks are doing fine. Lucy has a little girl about two or three years old.

I'm getting so sleepy I can hardly hold my eyes open so I'll close for now. Write often.

Love to all
Charles

(Passed by Naval Sensors)

U.S.S. LCI (L) No. 42

February 26, 1944

Dear Pop,

Yours of a recent date received and greatly enjoyed. Glad to hear that everything is O.K. Too bad about Sue's illness but it's good that she has it over with and well on the road to recovery. It seems that the medical profession has the appendectomy just about down to the level of tooth extraction these days.

How are the "boys" behaving? Are you getting any work out of them? Guess you're glad to see Spring coming since it will mean no more firewood for a while. Are you planning to put in much of a crop?

How is Grandpa's health holding up? I think of him often and long for some of his 'coon tales. Hope he will still be able to spin some for me when I get back. Remember me to him.

How does the situation over here look from the outside? It's a tough fight but I think we can make it. As Churchill says, we've got to fight their army some place so this is as good as any, I suppose. We are all looking forward to the big push across the channel but know nothing of the plans. And we often speculate on the possibilities of our participating in it—and that we know nothing about either. It's going to be a good show and I would hate to miss it. Let's hope that, at any rate, this Summer will see the end of the "Kraut."

I am reading a book now that I believe you would find very interesting. It's "The Apostle" by Sholem Asch and concerns the life of Paul. It is very well written and the author shows great knowledge of what life must have been like back in those days. It is written, however, as a novel and should be read as one. Another very good one I read some time ago was "The Robe" which dealt with the fellow who won Christs Robe after he was crucified and how, through a long chain of interesting adventures, it brought about his conversion. Some of the places I have seen over here have created within me a deep interest in Biblical history and I have been doing some quite extensive reading along that line during recent months.

Do you get any of the news magazines? There is an article in the Feb. 7 issue of "Time" about the Anzio beach head & a Lt. Col John Toffee which I found very interesting. I know the col. very well—will tell you about it sometime.

I'm beginning to look forward now to my next promotion. It should get it by July if something unexpected doesn't come up. It will mean a little more financially than the last one.

Well, hold everything down there and we'll have this little job over here done for you pretty soon. Write me when you find time.

Affectionately,
Prof.

3

over here have created within me a deep interest in Biblical history and I have been doing some quite extensive reading along that line during recent months.

Do you get any of the news magazines? There is an article in the Feb 1 issue of "Time" about the Anzio beach head & a Lt. Col. John Toffee which I found very interesting. I know the col. very well— will tell you about it sometime.

I'm beginning to look forward now to my next promotion. It should get it by July if something unexpected doesn't come up. It will mean a little more financially than the last one.

Well, hold everything down there and we'll have this little job over here done for you pretty soon. Write me when you find time.

Affectionately,

Prof.

DELPHIE'S TRUNK

(Passed by Naval Sensors)

U.S.S. LCI (L) No. 42

April 11, 1944

Dear Mama,

I'm awfully sorry that I haven't been able to write for several days—just one of those things that can't be helped. Everything is O.K. and I'm feeling fine. Hope you are all well.

I haven't heard from you for several days but, on the whole, our mail is coming through much better now. I received a box of candy from you about a week ago but the razor and blades have not come through yet. I also got the box of Hershey's from Helen.

What did you do on Easter Sunday. Mine was just another day—my second Easter overseas.

I guess the trout season will open this coming Saturday. It will be the third one in a row that I have missed. I sure am going to have a lot to make up for when I get back.

I'll bet the kids really have grown. School will soon be over and you should be able to get some good work out of them this Summer.

Helen wrote me about the expected addition to the family. I think it is a good idea but I hope Roy isn't called away before she is straightened out again. And be sure that she comes home well in advance of the time. She is very lonesome there.

Am enclosing a picture of Jim and I but don't examine too closely the expression on my face! Didn't know I was a tank driver, did you?

Remember me to everyone and write often.

Love,
Charles

(Passed by Naval Sensors)

U.S.S. LCI (L) No. 42

April 11, 1944

Dear Daddy,

I have been very slow in getting around to answering your letter for which I am sorry. Business has been rather rushing.

Mama wrote about your *"Shonny Haw" deal. Sounds like some good money in it. Wish I were there to help you. About three months of that kind of life would be just the thing for me right now.

Was very glad to hear about your buying the Piano for Ducky. I'm sure you will all derive a great deal of pleasure from it (that is, after the kids become well enough accustomed to it so that they don't fight over it.)

It will be a pleasure to furnish you the "cow money" but it will take a couple of months (Perhaps the last of June) for me to get it clear. My bank account is a "savings account" you know and just at the present my pocket account is rather low. But it will come through in time.

How's the old Ford hitting these days? Do you have any trouble keeping her in tires and gasoline?

I think I am about to break a family tradition—I'm slowly growing bald. I'll be a "peach" when that happens, too but I don't know what I can do about it. Perhaps it will add distinction if nothing else.

Everything is about the same with me. Can't complain about a thing, I guess.

Write when you find time.

Affectionately—Son

*Tree bark used to make medicinal tea

V - MAIL

(Passed by Naval Sensors)

U.S.S. LCI (L) No. 42
14 April, 1944

Dear Mama,

Just a few lines to let you know that everything is O.K. The mail isn't coming through as well now. I got a V-Mail from you yesterday, the only letter I have had in a week.

No, the razor and blades haven't come yet but don't worry about it—they'll come. Packages are very slow in getting here. I have been using my electric razor which serves the purpose even though I don't like it.

The coca-cola idea really sounds good. Hope you are successful in finding them and getting them in the mail.

My love to all of you.

Always
Charles

AMERICAN RED CROSS SERVICE CLUB

April 15, 1944

Dear Mama,

Well, today, it happened—I knew it was bound to sooner or later. I was bringing the ship into dock and the first line was hardly over when a soldier came up on the bridge and shouted "Charles." And who should it be but Haskel Hall. And was I glad to see him!

We had about three hours together and he had dinner with me. He has been over eighteen months and I have been here thirteen and neither of us had seen a single person from home since we left (except Tom, of course).

You have no idea how my morale is boosted. And now that I know where he is, I think I can see him rather often. Martha Lee had written him and given my address. Haskel told me how I might get in touch with Walt McNeely so I may be seeing him soon.

I think I will write Haskel's folks that I saw him and he's well but if I don't get around to it, you might try to let them know.

He has really been through the thick of it and we have been in several fights together if we had only known about it. In fact, I have walked right by the place he is staying now several times. He seems to be taking it in good style and his health is "in the pink."

Haskel had a letter from J.C. Owen recently and he is near-by. There is a good chance that I may be able to look him up. J.C., also, is in a fighting outfit.

AMERICAN RED CROSS SERVICE CLUB

Someone had written Haskel that Daddy was going to write him a letter and he's been looking forward to it. So if Daddy hasn't already done so, tell him to please write him right away. He says he will write to you folks soon.

I had an air mail letter from you yesterday and one from Helen. Glad to hear that everything is going O.K. I'm doing fine.

Some months ago an Army Captain who was a passenger took a picture of some of the crew. He was on his way home and after he got there he had some developed and sent us several copies. I think they are very good. Please keep this one for me because I want to have some enlargements made when I get back. We were just off the beach so the uniforms aren't exactly up to regulation but they very seldom are when men are in a fight.

We have just received word from several sources that the "Fightin' 42" has appeared in several movie news reels back home recently as she was disgorging troops on a certain beach.

Guess that's all for now. Best wishes to all.

Love
Charles

AMERICAN RED CROSS SERVICE CLUB

off the beach so the uniforms aren't exactly up to regulation but they very seldom are where men are in a fight.

We have just received word from several sources that the "Fightin' 42" has appeared in several movie news reels back home recently as she was disgorging troops on a certain beach.

Guess that's all for now. Best wishes to all.

Love
Charles

(Passed by Naval Sensors)

U.S.S. LCI (L) No. 42
May 6, 1944

Dear Mama,

Writing has been difficult for the past few weeks and may become more so soon. However, don't worry yourself about me because everything is O.K.

The packages have been coming through this week. I got the razor and blades, the shick blades and two boxes of candy and some razor blades from Helen so I'm all fixed now. Thanks a million.

I had a v-mail from John recently but he didn't give me any idea of his location. I noticed his address contained an A.P.O. so he was either leaving soon or already on his way.

I've seen Haskel a couple more times since I last wrote. He is O.K. I wonder if you will help me out of a very embarrassing situation. Is Haskel's mother still living? I'm ashamed of myself for not knowing but I can't seem to remember.

I am enclosing a couple of pictures we had made a couple of days ago by a street photographer. I think they are pretty good but am afraid they will eventually fade out—they were developed and printed in twenty minutes. Don't you think you have a very handsome son? Ahem!

I ran into a fellow I was in college with the other day. Mack Fore from Candler—you can probably find him in one of my annuals. We had a happy reunion. He's a Sgt. In the Army.

Tom isn't around here any more. Rumor has him in England—lucky stiff.

I got the Asheville paper with mine and John's picture in it.

I haven't seen Jim Galloway in some-time but expect to see him soon. He has been promoted to Major recently. My next promotion is due at the end of this month. When it comes I expect a transfer soon thereafter but it will probably be to something else over here. The Admiral says he would be a poor coach if he pulled his quarterback out in the middle of the game. So you see there is little hope in my getting home soon.

My love to all and write often.

Always,
Charles

(Passed by Naval Sensors)

U.S.S. LCI (L) No. 42

May 11, 1944

Dear Mama,

I have had no mail since I last wrote but expect some real soon—perhaps tomorrow. Hope everyone is well.

Sorry I couldn't send you and Dan a birthday present. There are lots of things over here to buy but they are sold at about four times what you would pay back home and then there is the risk you run in mailing them. Has the box I mailed arrived yet?

It seems that another Summer has rolled around. I have already been swimming several times and have a pretty good tan started.

I am going around "Starry eyed" these days because of a certain little Italian gal by the name of Isabella. She is really wonderful and speaks perfect English. Her father is Mayor of a certain city and they have a beautiful home. There is just one catch in the deal and that is the Italian custom of not permitting young ladies to go any place unchaperoned. So any place at all I take her, I also have to take Mama or Papa along. However, they are very good sports so we get along fine. Courting an Italian girl is just like the old days, you know, the boy and girl sat in one corner of the parlor and Mama, with her knitting, in the other. But it's lots of fun to sneak things, you know!

What do you hear from John? I haven't heard anything since I last wrote you.

Am enclosing a picture we had made at the beach a few days ago. Guess that's all for now.

Love,
Charles

UNITED STATES NAVY

(Passed by Naval Sensors)

U.S.S. LCI (L) No. 42

14 May 1944

Dear Mama,

I think of you most all the time but more than usual today because it is Mother's Day.

I wish I could express some of the thoughts and feelings I have had today and tell you in some little way just how much you mean to me. I would also like to express my thanks for all you have done. Any attempt at such a task, however, would be so inadequate that I shant try. I will say that if I have ever accomplished anything worthwhile or done anything that made you proud and happy, it was done to repay you in a small way.

One of Longfellow's passages has been running through my mind all morning. I would like to quote it for you but I'm afraid I have been away from my books too long. It concerned the effect of a letter from his mother and went something like this. "I derive more moral courage and more determination to do the right and live a clean life in one letter from my mother than from all the books, lectures, and sermons in all the world." And it's true. Your absolute faith in me, your encouraging words and words of praise have done more toward making me what I am than anything in all the world. I just hope that I can always justify that faith.

I think I can understand a little of what you are going through now and to me that is one of the most tragic parts of the war. We don't mind our part in it but more than anything else we feel for our mothers back home. And I think it is them more than anything else that we have in mind when we have a chance to do something to bring it all to an end.

It won't be too long, Mama. So just keep faith and wait and one Mothers day soon we will celebrate in Peace.

Your loving son
Charles

14 May 1944

Dear Mama,

I think of you most all the time but more than usual today because it is Mother's Day.

I wish I could express some of the thoughts and feelings I have had today and tell you in some little way just how much you mean to me. I would also like to express my thanks for all you have done. Any attempt at such a task, however, would be so inadequate that I shant try. I will say that if I have ever accomplished anything worthwhile or done anything that made you proud and happy, it was done to repay you in a small way.

One of Longfellow's passages has been running through my mind all morning. I would like to quote it for you but I'm afraid I have been away from my books too long. It concerned the effect of a letter from his mother and went something like this. "I derive more moral courage and more determination to do the right and live a clean life in one letter from my mother than from all the books, lectures, and sermons in all the world." And it's true. Your absolute faith in me, your encouraging words and words of praise have done more toward making me what I am than anything in all the world. I just hope that I can always justify that faith.

I think I can understand a little of what you are going through now and to me that is one of the most tragic parts of the war. We don't mind our part in it but more than anything else we feel for our mothers back home. And I think it is them more than anything else that we have in mind when we have a chance to do something to bring it to an end.

It won't be too long, Mama. So just keep faith and wait and one mothers day soon we will celebrate in Peace.

your loving son
Charles

(Passed by Naval Sensors)

U.S.S. LCI (L) No. 42

22 May 1944

Dear Mama,

I have time for just a note to let you know that everything is O.K. I'm pretty busy these days but getting enough sleep and rest.

I haven't heard from you for some time. The "Spuds" came and thanks. Also I got three coca-colas which I enjoyed more than anything I've had in months.

I had a letter from Daddy a few days ago which I plan to answer soon.

How are the crops coming? You must have quite a bit.

Nothing much to write about so I'll close. Will write more soon.

Love,
Chas

(Passed by Naval Sensors)

U.S.S. LCI (L) No. 42

May 25, 1944

Dear Pop,

Your recent letter concerning Helen's future disposition has been received and given due consideration.

I am thoroughly in agreement on the fact that she should be there with you folks and have told her so several times in recent letters. But I also agree that if I were Roy, I would assume the same attitude he has taken. Therefore, as far as we are concerned, it is a problem. Tonight, I have written them again suggesting that she get down there before the Summer becomes too hot. And suggestion, I believe, is as far as any of us should, or can, go. The arguments you presented are good ones but should I present them to him, I'm afraid he would receive them with more resentment than reason. A man's wife is his own property, you know, and besides that I am sure that he must already realize the advantages in sending her down there. So, as I said before, suggestion is as far as I feel justified in going at the present time. You know the situation far better than I, however, so if you feel that I should do something more, please tell me so. But even if they decide that she shall remain in Baltimore, I don't think there is too much cause for worry because I'm sure she will receive adequate attention and care. Let's all hope for the best.

How's the shonny haw business coming along? I was surprised when Mama wrote that you had taken Jerry and Dan along with you on a trip. They must really be grown up men by now. Of course, I remember when I used to go with you on the same missions. My greatest goal was the trip to Asheville to sell it and I imagine theirs is the same.

There have been no radical changes in my set-up. I'm getting a little more time off for rest and relaxation than usual and, believe me, I'm taking advantage of every minute of it. Ordinarily I wouldn't do it but I've been going for so long that I feel it is justified. I haven't had a leave now in 20 months (excluding the couple of days at Christmas '42).

I shall soon be able to send you the "cow money." Having been away so long, however, I am at a loss to know just how much you need—I understand prices are sky-high. I want you to get a good one and a few dollars don't mean anything. Is $125 about right?

I always enjoy your letters immensely so whenever you have a chance, drop me a line.

Affectionately

Prof.

(Passed by Naval Sensors)

U.S.S. LCI (L) No. 42

May 31, 1944

Dear Mama,

It has been several days since I had a chance to write but am getting along fine. Our mail is coming through pretty slowly now and I find it hard to write when I don't get letters. I did get one V-Mail from you yesterday which had been mailed on May 20 which I thought made very good time.

Glad to hear that the box and pictures arrived. You asked about the things in the box and I have almost forgotten what there was in it. The only things I want for myself are the tan gloves, the bracelet & necklace set and the little things you mentioned. The rest of it you may do with as you please. If there is enough to go around, try to give everyone something.

I guess I should mail you folks more souvenirs but these Italians really "soak" you for things like that so I don't buy much. And anyway, most of the things they have to sell can be bought back home for one tenth the price you pay here. And what makes me mad is that they make suckers out of us. Money doesn't mean much to the fellows over here and the "Ities" really take advantage of that fact.

Something is in the air for a transfer for me but I don't know what to. I may be made engineering officer of the flotilla in which case I won't get home for many months. On the other hand there is a *very* slight possibility that I will get home soon. I don't dare make any predictions as to what will happen and it makes little difference to me one way or the other. I would like to get home for a little while but after that I might get an assignment I wouldn't like and too, I hate to leave the other guys over here. We have a tip-top outfit of which we are all very proud.

I've got to get some sleep now because I'm going to be up most of the night. Give my love to everyone.

Always,
Charles

(Passed by Naval Sensors)

U.S.S. LCI (L) No. 42

June 5, 1944

Dear Mama,

Your letter of May twenty fourth telling of the Pettit episode came today along with one from Alice.

I can see where you found yourself in a rather peculiar situation but I can't keep from laughing at it just a little. Mama, I actually believe you are getting old and childish—(I'm still laughing) for otherwise how could the matter of whether or not we have "made up" make any difference about you showing her the things and talking to her. I'm out of the "Puppy love" stage, Mama and I have no secrets to keep from Alice and even if we have broken up, we'll always be good friends. Please don't misunderstand me, Mama, I'm not being "snoty" nor am I laughing at you—it's just a funny situation, that's all. I know just how you felt and it was all for me which I appreciate but it was unnecessary. I have no secrets to keep from anyone and I just don't care enough to go out of my way to make impressions or influence people. So please don't worry about it.

Quite a letter I had from Alice today. She said some awfully nice things about you folks and, my goodness, at the other things she said! Guess I should play "hard to get" and let her worry for a while but for some reason or other I can't. I'm afraid I like her quite a bit and she is awfully sweet. So you might say that everything is "honey & sugar" again. Guess this boy of yours is kind of hard to understand, isn't he? He'll make out.

Hope everyone is well and happy. I'm doing fine but the weather is terribly hot. Love to all

Always,
Charles

(Passed by Naval Sensors)

U.S.S. LCI (L) No. 42

16 June 1944

Dear Mama,

Just a few lines to let you know that everything is O.K. How is everyone there?

In your last letter you asked about the cigarettes. Yes the both came and the coca-colas are coming through fine. Thanks. I can think of nothing I need particularly right at the present.

I had a letter from Ducky recently and one from Sue. Will answer them as soon as I can find time.

The Kraut is on the run and we're busy keeping him running. Don't worry if you don't hear from me too often.

Love to all
Charles

(Passed by Naval Sensors)

U.S.S. LCI (L) No. 42

June 21, 1944

Dear Mama & Daddy,

Needless to say that the news of John was a terrible shock. I sincerely hope that he is safe and that news to that effect will reach us soon. So many of the fellows I know over here have had friends and relatives reported missing and later listed as prisoners that it gives me much hope for John.

I know the suspense for both of you is terrible and I wish I could do something or say something to make it a little easier, and John would too. Wherever he is, his greatest concern is for you folks. So please try to keep your chins up and hope for the best. I know you will.

For your sakes, I had so earnestly hoped that the war would never come so close to you and that you would never have to realize the terribleness of it. God knows you have never done anything to deserve it. But the world is in an awful mess—I never realized how awful until I saw some of it and listened to some of the experiences of others. Now all we can do is give our all in trying to get it set right again. And thank God, in our case, the young men can take the blunt of it instead of innocent women and children. So whatever any of us have to give we can rest assured that the cause for which we give it is perfectly worthy. I know that it's next to impossible to forget the personal side of it but other peoples have had to so let us go as far as we can in doing it before it is forced upon us.

The thing that has happened to us has happened to millions. So let us, like they have, take renewed determination that the lousey heathen who started this shall pay for it ten fold.

I send to each of you a very personal message of sympathy, a plea for continued hope, and a promise of revenge and victory. It won't be too much longer until this will be over for good.

Mama, don't worry too much. Your boys have to face the world sooner or later and though I admit this is a pretty tough one to face, we can do it and without a whimper. Try to find comfort and have faith in your prayers. Everything will be alright.

Hope everyone is well. I'm doing fine, eating good, and not working too hard.

Love to all
Charles

June 21, 1944

Dear Mama + Daddy,

Needless to say that the news of John was a terrible shock. I sincerely hope that he is safe and that news to that effect will reach us soon. So many of the fellows I know over here have had friends and relatives reported missing and later listed as prisoners that it gives me much hope for John.

I know the suspense for both of you is terrible and I wish I could do something or say something to make it a little easier. And John would too. Wherever he is, his greatest concern is for you folks. So please try to keep your chins up and hope for the best. I know you will.

For your sakes, I had so earnestly hoped that the war would never come so close to you and that you would never have to realize the terribleness of it. God knows you have never done anything to deserve it. But the world is in an awful mess — I never realized how awful until I saw some of it and listened to some of the experiences of others. Now all we can do is give our all in trying to get it set right again. And thank God, in our case, the young men can take the brunt of it instead of innocent women and children. So whatever any of us have to give we can rest assured that the cause for which we give it is perfectly worthy. I know that it's next to impossible to forget the personal side of it but other peoples have had to so let us go as far as we can in doing it before it is forced upon us.

The thing that has happened to us has happened to millions. So let us, like they have, take renewed determination that the lousy heathen who started this shall pay for it ten fold.

I send to each of you a very personal message of sympathy, a plea for continued hope, and a promise of revenge and victory. It won't be too much longer until this will be over for good.

Mama, don't worry too much. Your boys have to face the world sooner or later and though I admit this is a pretty tough one to face, we can do it and without a whimper. Try to find comfort and have faith in your prayers. Everything will be alright.

Hope everyone is well. I'm doing fine, eating good, and not working too hard.

Love to all
Charles

Mrs. C.W. Mallonee
Candler, N.C.

July 2nd (1944)

Dear Mrs. McCall:

I noticed in the paper that S.Sgt. Carlos McCall was a German prisoner. I wonder if he could be your son, am so sorry if it is would you let me know. I hear from Charlie through his girl Sally Watson of Columbus Ohio. Tom has a girl up there so she writes me. Am proud of Charlies new rating. I guess Tom has the same, but he is in England, had a cablegram from him last night the first I have heard since the invasion. Was so happy to hear from him. Hope your family is well, and let me hear from you.

Sincerely
Mrs. C.W. Mallonee

July 2 40.

Dear Mrs McCall,

I noticed in the paper that S. Sgt Carlos McCall was a German prisoner. I wonder if he could be your son. am so sorry if it is would you let me know. I hear from Charlie through his girl Sally Watson of Columbus Ohio. Tom has a girl up there to so she writes me. am proud of Charlies new rating. I guess Tom has the same, but he is in England, had a cablegram from him last night the first I have heard since the invasion. was so happy to hear from him. Hope your family is well. and let me hear from you

Sincerely

Mrs C. W. Mallow

(Passed by Naval Sensors)

U.S.S. LCI (L) No. 42

July 5, 1944

Dear Mama,

Your letter of May 21 came yesterday. Was glad to hear that everyone is well. I'm doing fine—just getting over a head cold that has been rather bother-some for a few days.

Another box of coca-colas came today and I just finished one. They sure are good.

The Fourth of July was rather quiet around here. It was just another day for me. Hope yours was nice.

I saw Mack Fore again yesterday for just a little while. I'm not too far away from Jim Galloway now and plan to look him up soon.

Some time ago I had quite a bit of time in Rome. I found it very beautiful and as interesting as most anything I've seen over here. Among the things I saw was the old Roman Forum, the Colleseum and the other Roman ruins, Mussilini's balcony and forum, The Vatican City & The Pope, St. Peter's tomb and contains as much gold as a mint. I was also in the prison where St. Peter & Paul were kept.

Sure hope you get some news of John soon.

Will close for now. Love to all

Always
Charles

(Passed by Naval Sensors)

U.S.S. LCI (L) No. 42

July 12, 1944

Dear Mama,

Sure was glad to get the news about John. I am not able to write him from here but can send you a letter to mail for me. I plan to do that real soon.

Jim Galloway was by to see me a few nights ago and we had a happy reunion. We are only a few miles apart but both seem to be so busy that we can't get together.

Our mail isn't coming through so well now but I expect it to get better soon. Had a nice long letter from Helen yesterday.

Everything is fine with me. Hope you are all well. Write often.

Love,
Charles

(Passed by Naval Sensors)

LT. CHARLES A. McCALL, U.S.N.R.
U.S.S. L.C.I. (L) NO. 42
c/o FLEET POST OFFICE, NEW YORK, N.Y.

July 29, 1944

Dear Mama,

The stationary certainly is nice and I was beginning to need some rather badly. So I certainly appreciate it and thank you.

Our mail still seems to be fouled up somewhere. The last letter I got from you was the one containing the pictures. I think they are very good. It kind of reminds me how long I have been away when I see how much the kids have grown.

I have submitted a request for transfer to some position of more responsibility and it has been approved. For certain reasons which I can't mention here, however, it is being help up for a few weeks. As I have said before, I have no idea as to what or where it will be but hope I can get home for a little while.

The former Skipper who is now in Texas sent me a set of Lt. collar bars and I bought some shoulder boards over here so I'm all decorated up with my new rank. Let's hope that before the season for blues comes around that I'll be home and you can put my stripes on.

Sure hope you have had some word from John before now and that everything is well with him. If these Russians keep going we'll see him soon. The news sure is good now.

If you don't hear from me for a spell, don't worry about it. Give everyone my love and write often.

Always
Charles

AIR MAIL

UNITED STATES OF AMERICA
AIR MAIL
6 CENTS

Mrs. Clyde A. McCall
Lake Toxaway,
North Carolina

LT. CHARLES A. MCCALL. U.S.N.R.
U.S.S. L. C. I. (L) NO 42
C/O FLEET POST OFFICE, NEW YORK, N. Y.

PASSED BY NAVAL CENSOR

(Passed by Naval Sensors)

LT. CHARLES A. McCALL, U.S.N.R.
U.S.S. L.C.I. (L) NO. 42
c/o FLEET POST OFFICE, NEW YORK, N.Y.

August 9, 1944

Dear Mama,

How is everyone? I haven't heard from you in some time. The only mail we have had recently was a bunch of packages but I did O.K. I got the second box of stationery, the fruitcake and chewing gum, and three coca-colas. It was all good and thanks a million.

I see now that writing this letter is going to be most difficult. The other officers are beginning a discussion of the possibilities of life on the planets and that always gets me.

I have been seeing quite a bit of Jim Galloway recently and we've had quite a bit of fun. We are both hoping to get home soon.

Have you heard from John yet. I sure would like to know how he is. I don't believe it will be too long until we will have him back again. How is Doris.

Guess what I had for dinner today. Corn on the cob. And was it good. I miss that more than most anything else along the eating line.

I'm going to have to give this up before I get onto the canals on Mars. I doing fine and will write again at the first opportunity. It may be some time. Love to all

Always
Charles

(Passed by Naval Sensors)

LT. CHARLES A. McCALL, U.S.N.R.
U.S.S. L.C.I. (L) NO. 42
c/o FLEET POST OFFICE, NEW YORK, N.Y.

September 9, 1944

Dear Mama,

Your V-Mail of August 21 came today and was glad to hear that everyone is well. Sounds like you got a good buy in the cow. I can't wait for some good cold sweet milk—I've had one glass in eighteen months now.

Was very happy to hear that Helen and the baby are doing nicely—of course, I had hoped for boy. She sent me some pictures of Suzanne recently and I could hardly believe it was her. She certainly has grown.

I have finally found a place which I think is more beautiful than Western North Carolina—Southern France. It certainly is wonderful—and the women!

Things will be settling down again pretty soon and I will start looking for my transfer. Still some possibility that I might get home.

It's hard to understand why you haven't heard more from John—however, I imagine that communications (including mail services) are very limited in the Reich right now. Deplorable situation, to say the least.

I have often mentioned in my letters what a good outfit we have over here and how proud we are of it. Am enclosing a short clipping from "Time" magazine to show what some other people think of us. Guess practice does make perfect after all.

Give everyone my love and I'll be seeing you.

Always
Charles

(Passed by Naval Sensors)

U.S.S. LCI (L) No. 42

September 20, 1944

Dear Mama,

It has been so long since we had any mail that I find it hard to write. There is always so little to write about.

"The best laid plans of mice & men—". I thought that surely by now my transfer would be through but we are in such a position now that I can't expect it for some time. And as long as there is work to do I don't mind.

There certainly is some beautiful country here and I never miss a chance to get ashore and enjoy some of it. It reminds me quite a bit of home in a lot of respects.

Hope everyone is well there. What have you heard from John? Guess the kids are starting back to school. Give everyone my love.

Always
Charles

UNITED STATES NAVY

AMPHIBIOUS TRAINING BASE
LITTLE CREEK, VIRGINIA

December 13, 1944

Dear Mama,

Alice told me that you had had only one letter from me. I can't understand that. Neither can I understand why I have had only two from you. Sure hope the situation will improve soon.

Since you have had only one letter, you probably know very little about the set-up here. Neither do I but I'll tell you what I know. It seems that when I came there was no openings in the program for an engineer of my rank. Hence I was assigned as prospective commanding officer of an L.S.M. I immediately wrote the Bureau of Personell for a change of orders which I probably will not get. And if not, I'll be here for two or three months in training after which I will get my ship. The ship will stick around for a couple of months then we'll head out. I already have my crew and officers (four officers and sixty men) and we are more or less training together. That is the set-up, a change is possible but not probably.

Guess I won't get home for Christmas but will have a few days (3 or 4) about the middle of January at which time Alice and I plan to be married. We are both so sick over our decision to put it off that we have decided not to let another opportunity pass. Very tentatively, the wedding will be at Brevard Baptist Church on the afternoon of Friday, January 19. Guess I'm finally hooked, Mama.

Hope everyone is well and looking forward to a Merry Christmas. I will have a half day off and a good meal so I guess mine will be pretty good. Haven't done any shopping yet but hope to get around to it soon.

Give my love to everyone and I'll try to write more often after this.

Love,
Charles

P.S. Let me know when you hear from John.

AMPHIBIOUS TRAINING BASE
LITTLE CREEK, VIRGINIA

December 13, 1944

Dear Mama,

Alice told me that you had had only one letter from me. I can+ understand that. Neither can I understand why I have had only two from you. Sure hope the situation will improve soon.

Since you have had only one letter, you probably know very little about the set-up here. Neither do I but I'll tell you what I know. It seems that when I came there was no openings in the program for an engineer of my rank. Hence I was assigned as prospective commanding officer of an L.S.M. I immediately wrote the Bureau of personell for a change of orders which I probably will not get. And if not, I'll be here for two or three months in training after which I will get my ship. The ship will stick around for a couple of months then we'll head out. I already have my crew and officers (four officers and sixty men) and we are more or less training together. That is the set-up. A change is possible but not probable.

Guess I won't get home for Christmas but will have a few days (3 or 4) about the middle of January at which time Alice and I plan to be married. We are both so sick over our decision to put it off that we have decided not to let another opportunity pass. Very tentatively, the wedding will be at Buford Baptist church on the afternoon of Friday, January 19. Guess I'm finally hooked, Mama.

Hope everyone is well and looking forward to a Merry Christmas. I will have a half day off and a good meal so I guess mine will be pretty good. Haven't done any shopping yet but hope to get around to it soon.

Give my love to everyone and I'll try to write more often after this.

Love,
Charles

P.S. Let me know when you hear from John.

Dan McCall and Jerry McCall
Lake Toxaway, N.C.

Lt. Charles A. McCall
Unit 1130 Div. & A.T.B.
Little Creek, V.A.

Dec 25, 1944

Dear Charles,

We have to be quiet now. Because Doris and her baby is here But we don't mind it. She is going home tomorrow. I hope she comes back pretty soon. Her baby is so cute I can't keep my hands away from him.

Alice gave Joe Ben a wartank it was in a box like some—crackers. So we teased him yesterday about Alice getting him a box of soda crackers for a present. And he believe us at first but Alice told him better this morning when he opened—it this morning he was relly was surprised. I got a pair of overall pants and a cotton shirt and a sweater and some other things dan got the same. And we both got two model airplanes sets. Helen sent us one and Santa Claus brought us one. We had some fun at school. Daddy gave a boy a pair of Rotts ____ teeth that uncle Homer gave me to give to mama for a joke about two years ago. So daddy _____ them up. When Daddy was giving out the present he and said is Forest Chapman. He pulled the false teeth out everybody started laughing they laugh for about five minutes. You outh to have seen the crowd around his desk. When they all went back to their desk he said Old Mr. McCall gave me them teeth. I made out like I didn't hear him.

So I guess I had better close.

Your brother
Jerry

December 25

Dear Charles,

I was just a line to tell you that I was all right. I hope that you can be home by New Years.

    Joeben was just fussing at Mama because she would not get his candle. Dorris baby is crying so that I can't think of anything to right. I guess I will have to close.

Your brother
Dan

You my Call and Jury
Lake toxavoary n.c.

Lt. Charles C. McCall
unit 1130 Air. 7 ans. B.
Little Creek, V.a.

CHAPTER ELEVEN

Marriage, Ft. Pierce and Japan

The engagement announcement of Alice Winifred Pettit and Lt. Charles Allen McCall appeared in the Christmas Eve 1944 edition of the *Transylvania Times*. He gave her a beautiful one carat diamond engagement ring set in yellow gold. I didn't know until Aunt Sue mentioned it a few years before she died, that there was an engagement party for them. Some of the family was having dinner with Sue at a BBQ restaurant on the outskirts of town, which used to be the Brevard Country Club. At one point she looked around the large dining room and said, "This is where your Mama and Daddy had their engagement party." I wish I had asked about the details, but I didn't. I do remember thinking that this must have been a perfect space for a 1940's celebration, rustically beautiful, log cabin like with high ceilings, a giant fireplace, and a huge hardwood dance floor. I imagine it was quite an evening for the happy couple. Alice and Charles were married on January 13, 1945 at the First Baptist Church in Brevard, North Carolina. A reception followed at her parent's home on Park Avenue. Their life as newlyweds is described in this chapter of letters which span the year 1945.

1945 was an eventful year which saw an end to World War II. On the twelfth of April President Roosevelt died. The nation mourned openly and profoundly for this iconic statesman who had led our country out of The Great Depression, through Pearl Harbor and thus far WWII. His comforting and inspirational "fireside chats" fell silent on radios across the America. Upon

FDR's death, Vice-President Harry S. Truman became President and Commander-in Chief. By the end of April, Mussolini had been murdered in Italy and Hitler had committed suicide in Germany. V-E Day (Victory in Europe) came on May 8, 1945. The war continued with Japan. In mid-July Allied leaders met in Germany and repeated their demand for Japan's unconditional surrender stating: "the alternative for Japan is prompt and utter destruction." There was no surrender. In August President Truman issued an executive order for the dropping of atomic bombs on two Japanese cities, Hiroshima on August 6th and Nagasaki on August 9th. Thousands upon thousands of Japanese civilians were killed. It was horrific and the ethical justification for the use of nuclear weapons is still debated. However, President Truman's difficult decision brought about the official surrender of Japan to the Allies on September 2, 1945. After six years and one day, World War II was finally and mercifully over. Sixty **million** Allied lives, both military and civilian, had been lost.

Imagine having all of the above happen during your first year of marriage. Well, that is exactly what Grandpa Charlie and Grandma Alice experienced during 1945. And if that weren't enough, John was still a German prisoner of war when these letters begin. By the end of the year, Navy duty in the Pacific would separate these newlyweds again.

(Wedding Poem)*

A nation was born on July Four
A war ended November Eleven
An on December Twenty Five
Our Christ came down from Heaven.

These symbolic dates might well
Have come on other days
But since they happened when they did
Their symbolism stays.

Every day that passes by
For some has special meaning
And for each of us there's a special day
For memories and for dreaming.

The most important date for me
Is not New Year's nor Christmas
But the anniversary of that day
You gave to me your promise.

Today's that day and as I dream
Of that one when you tied me
I'm thrilled because not only is
It the thirteenth but Friday.

*This must be a draft of the poem Grandpa Charlie
gave to Grandma Alice on their wedding day,
January 13, 1945.

VS ~ WOMEN'S ACT

Miss Pettit Is Wedded To Lt. C. A. McCall

BREVARD—Miss Alice Winifred Pettit, daughter of Mr. and Mrs. J. B. Pettit, of Brevard, became the bride of Lt. Charles A. McCall, of Lake Toxaway, in a candlelight ceremony at the Brevard First Baptist church, Saturday evening, January 13, at 7 o'clock.

The Rev. B. W. Thomason, pastor, officiated, in the presence of friends and relatives. The ring ceremony was used.

A motif of green and white, interspersed with calla lilies, formed the altar and other church decorations.

A program of organ music was given by Mrs. Melvin Gillespie, of Brevard. Before the ceremony, "Ave Maria" and "I Love You Truly" were sung by Miss Priscilla Lyon, of Brevard. The traditional wedding marches were played for the processional and recessional.

The bride, who was given in marriage by her father, wore a dress of white brocade satin, made princess style with sweetheart neckline. She wore a single strand of pearls. A fingertip veil ornamented her headdress. She carried a white Bible, topped with a spray of talisman roses.

Miss Eleanor Pettit, of Brevard, sister of the bride, was maid of honor. Her dress was of aqua brocade taffeta, fashioned princess style. Her flowers were calla lilies and white narcissi. Mrs. Robert Jackson, of Brevard, matron of honor, wore a dress of similar color and fashion as that of the maid of honor. Her bouquet was of white and yellow chrysanthemums.

T. C. McCall, of Lake Toxaway, cousin of the bridegroom, served as best man. C. F. Poole, Jr., and Glenn Winchester, of Brevard, were ushers.

An informal reception at the home of the bride's parents followed the ceremony. Miss Martha Jean Hardin and Miss Doris Wilson, of Brevard, assisted Mrs. Pettit in serving.

The couple is now at Fort Pierce, Fla., where Lieutenant McCall is stationed.

Mrs. McCall is a graduate of Brevard high school and attended the .... of South Carolina.

LT. AND MRS. C. A. McCALL—Miss Alice Winifred Pettit, daughter of Mr. and Hrs. J. B. Pettit of Brevard, became the bride of Lt. Charles A. McCall, son of Mr. and Mrs. Clyde A. McCall of Lake Toxaway, in a ceremony Saturday, January 13 in Brevard Baptist church.

MISS STELLA ROGERS WEDS CHARLES TATUM

ANDREWS—Mrs. Bertha Rogers of Andrews has announced the marriage of her daughter, Miss Stella Rogers to Charles D. Tatham of the United States navy, son of Mr. and Mrs. Claude Tatham of Andrews.

The marriage took place at Blairsville, Ga., Jan. 18. The couple was accompanied by Mr. and Mrs. David Tatham, Clarence Hogan and Horace Everett, all of Andrews.

✧ ✧ ✧

MRS. HAZEL SELF'S MARRIAGE ANNOUNCED

Only six holidays are legal in all the states and territories of the United States

A.T.B. *
Fort Pierce, Fla.
Jan. 20, 1945

Dear Mama,

Just a few lines to let you know that everything is fine. I was able to get a Pullman birth coming down so the trip wasn't bad at all. I had a two hour wait in Jacksonville so I called Tom and had breakfast with him. Sure was good seeing him again.

I think I'm going to like my work here fine. I have the electrical shop and a chance to study and learn something. I go to work at eight-thirty in the mornings and get off at five and night duty every eight of more days. The weather is wonderful. I go around the base in my shirt sleeves and nights are not cold enough for an overcoat. Hate to think of summer.

I rented us a house last night. It's a beautiful place but about eighteen miles away. It has a large living room, three bed rooms, two baths, a kitchen, dining room and sleeping porch. It's facing the sea and we'll have large lawns with our own private beach, pier and boat. A friend of mine and his wife will live with us and he has a car for driving to work. Rent is pretty high but any place costs like everything here.

Alice will arrive Tuesday afternoon and I can hardly wait. Guess everyone gets a kick out of their first try at housekeeping.

Give everyone my love and let me hear from you soon.

Always
Charles

*Amphibious Training Base

Lieut. Charles A. McCall
"The Crossroads"
Jensen Beach, Fla.
(Jan. 30, 1945)

Dear Mama,

A letter from you came yesterday but it was mailed before I was home and had been sent to Little Creek. I can't remember if I left my address with you or not but it was on my last letter. Our home address is at the top of the page.

With all the excitement and rush while I was home, I didn't get down to see Doris and the boy. It has worried me quite a bit wondering what she must think of me and I did want to see the boy. Hope she understands and will forgive me. Please send her address when you write and I will drop her a line.

Everything is fine here and we're getting along swell. Alice likes the house very much and since she has it to take care of the days won't seem quite so long. Both she and the other girl are wonderful cooks and I certainly am enjoying eating home cooking again. They buy the groceries and cook together and we split the expense. Things are working out fine so far.

Wish you could come down and enjoy this weather for a while. The days are rather hot and the nights just comfortable. We have a large fireplace in the house but have only used it one night so far.

Hope you are feeling better now and all the others are well. Write often for I miss you lots.

Love,
Charles

U.S. NAVAL AMPHIBIOUS
TRAINING BASE
FORT PIERCE, FLORIDA

"The Crossroads"
Jensen Beach, Fla.
Sunday
(Feb. 14, 1945)

Dear Mama,

Had a letter from you day before yesterday. Glad to hear that everyone is O.K. I, too, am wondering about John. It sure would be wonderful if he would show up one of these days. However, I guess we shouldn't expect too much.

Everything is swell with us and we're getting along fine. Alice is all excited about Bruce getting home and expects to go up for a few days soon, perhaps this week. I certainly hate to give her up for even a few days and also dread the trip for her but can understand how anxious she is to see Bruce.

Tell Daddy that I'm definitely on the market for an automobile now and it's almost impossible to find one here. If he can find anything let me know. We live about fifteen miles away from the base and five miles from any good sized town and need a car rather badly. Of course, there's several other officers who do have cars and we can arrange to go most anywhere but it isn't too good an arrangement.

I'm on duty tonight and things are very quite so I'm going to turn in early. Will write again soon.

As ever
Charles

"The Crossroads"
Jensen Beach, Fla.
Sunday

Dear Mama,

Had a letter from you day before yesterday.
Glad to hear that everyone is o.k. I, too, am
wondering about John. It sure would be
wonderful if he would show up one of these
days. However, I guess we shouldn't expect too
much.

Everything is swell with us and we're
getting along fine. Alice is all excited about some
getting home and expects to go up for a
few days soon, perhaps this week. I certainly
hate to give her up for even a few days
and also dread the trip for her but can
understand how anxious she is to see Bruce.

Tell Daddy that I'm definitely on the
market for an automobile now and it's
almost impossible to find one here. If he
can find anything let me know. We

Lieut. Charles A. McCall, U.S.N.R.
"The Crossroads"
Jensen Beach, Fla.

February 21, 1945

Dear Mama,

It's been several days since I wrote to you but since Alice was up to see you, you should have all the news anyway. She says that she gave you quite a surprise. And that surprises me because I thought I written you that she was coming.

Everything is fine here. I'm beginning to get a tan in the sunshine. I don't have very much time off but always like to get outside when I am.

I certainly was surprised at the news from Sue. I couldn't believe it for a while and still find it difficult to think of her as being married. Suppose you folks were surprised too.

The Brevard paper you sent came through O.K. Thanks. Alice says she has subscribed for us now.

Mrs. Pettit and Bruce will come tomorrow for a couple of days. I won't get to see much of them, I guess.

Am anxious for some word from John. Let me know as soon as you hear.

I noticed in the paper that Uncle Homer has been pretty sick again. How is he now?

I haven't heard from you in several days. Write when you have a chance.

Love,
Charles

UNITED STATES ATLANTIC FLEET
Amphibious Force

U. S. Naval Amphibious Training Base
Fort Pierce, Florida

27 February 1945

Dear Brooks,

I was very surprised the other day when I ran into Vest down here and he showed me a clipping from the Cincinatti paper which told of your return. It sure was swell news but I've been going around in circles ever since trying to fine out just what has happened. Why don't you let a guy in on the hot dope. Did you bring the old tub back? On the double there and let me hear from you.

McCall is a married man now—can you imagine that! And I must add that he is a very happy married man. It's quite the life, Brooksie, don't know how I've gotten along thus far without it.

I was up at Little Creek and all set to take an LSM out when out of a clear sky I got BuPers orders sending me here for duty in connection with base maintainence and repair. I've been here over a month now and certainly am pleased with the set-up. I am in charge of the electrical shop, have very decent hours and only one watch per week.

Mrs. McCall (how does that sound?) and I have a lovely little cottage on the beach and I certainly am enjoying my life there. Instead of finding McCall at some wild part every night, you will now find him at home in front of the fireplace with his pipe and beer while his wonderful little wife reads to him from a good book. I certainly am lucky and don't you think for a moment that I don't realize it.

A few days after I ran into Vest, I was out playing golf and as I was driving up to a green who do you thing should be putting but Hampton and Hyland. They have volunteered for some sort of super-secret and hazardous duty and are here training for it. Al Bellows is here on the same deal. Roger Frost is here connected with the receiving unit. Most of the officers who came back about the same time as I are on their way out now on LST's and LSM's.

I am anxious to hear where you wind up. I'm wishing you all the luck in getting something you will like. The last I heard from Lathrop was several weeks ago and he was still at Galveston. He expected to be sent out soon as operations officer for an LSM flotilla.

Remind me sometine to tell you about my wedding. The invasions were simple as compared to that—my knees were knocking home sweet home.

Sit down now and write to me—I'm very anxious to hear.

As ever,
Mac*

*Grandpa Charlie for as long as I can remember was called "Mac" by his colleagues.

UNITED STATES ATLANTIC FLEET
AMPHIBIOUS FORCE
U. S. NAVAL AMPHIBIOUS TRAINING BASE
FORT PIERCE, FLORIDA
27 February 1945

FILE No.
SERIAL:

Dear Brooks,

I was very surprised the other day when I ran into Vest down here and he showed me a clipping from the Cincinatti paper which told of your return. It sure was swell news but I've been going around in circles ever since trying to fine out just what has happened. Why don't you let a guy in on the hot dope. Did you bring the old tub back? On the double there and let me hear from you.

McCall is a married man now -- can you imagine that !! And I must add that he is a very happy married man. It's quite the life, Brooksie, don't know how I've gotten along thus far without it.

I was up at Little Creek and all set to take an LSM out when out of a clear sky I got BuPers orders sending me here for duty in connection with base maintainence and repair. I've been here over a month now and certainly am pleased with the set-up. I am in charge of the electrical shop, have very decent hours and only one watch per week.

Mrs. McCall (how does that sound?) and I have a lovely little cottage out on the beach and I certainly am enjoying my life there. Instead of finding McCall at some wild party every night, you will now find him at home in front of the fireplace with his pipe and a beer while his wonderful little wife reads to him from a good book. I certainly am lucky and don't you think for a moment that I don't realize it.

A few days after I ran into Vest, I was out playing golf and as I was driving up to a green who do you think should be putting but Hampton and Hyland. They havevolenteered for some sort of super-secret and hazardous duty and are here training for it. Al Bellows is here on the same deal. Roger Frost is here connected with the receiving unit. Most of the officers who came back about the same time as I are on their way out now on LST's and LSM's.

I am anxious to hear where you wind up. I'm wishing you all the luck in getting something you will like. The last I heard from Lathrop was several weeks ago and he was still at Galveston. He expected to be sent out soon as operations officer for an LSM flotilla.

Remind me sometime to tell you about my wedding. The invasions were simple as compared to that---my knees were knocking home sweet home.

Sit down now and write to me--I'm very anxious to hear.

As ever,

Lieut. Charles A. McCall, U.S.N.R.
"The Crossroads"
Jensen Beach, Fla.

                                                            14 March (1945)

Dear Mama,

It's been weeks since I heard from you. Hope everyone is well.

Sue hasn't written to me at all and I don't know where to write her. Please send me her address so I can write.

Have you heard anything from John recently. I notice that several prisoners have been liberated recently and I certainly hope he will make it soon.

I suppose that Spring will be coming there soon and I know you'll be glad. I don't look forward to it with so much pleasure as usual because it's going to be terribly hot here. The days are already beginning to get uncomfortable.

When Mrs. Pettit left I told her to tell you to try and locate me a ham. If you think it's safe to ship it, I'd still like to have one and will send you money for it if you can locate one.

Everything is fine with us. I am about to locate a more satisfactory place to live, I think, and if I am successful, we'll be moving within a few days. It certainly is next to impossible to find a decent place. We are very fond of the place have now but it's too far away from work and entirely too expensive.

I certainly have a good cook in Alice. I'm eating like a pig and gaining weight steadily. We are both very happy.

Do write often, Mama. I miss your letters when you don't and wonder about all of you. Give my love to all and tell the boys to write to me.

                                                            Love,
                                                            Charles

7 April 1945

Dear Homan,

I was very pleased at receiving your letter which arrived just this morning. It's always good to be remembered and I was glad for some news from you.

Sounds as though you landed yourself a darned good job. We are all happy for you and feel that Westinghouse is even luckier than you are as far as that deal is concerned. I'm sure it will be very interesting work and that you will enjoy it.

Needless to say that I have already missed you a dozen and one times. We have one diesel generator for battery charging now and are just getting ready to install it. Distribution board, panels, etc. will have to be designed and built. They are building us a generator room for that unit and two 30 K.W. A.C. jobs which we will also install.

Things go on about as usual here. Men are going out a little more rapidly and none are coming in. Robinson and several other of the older "veterans" around here are already gone. Chief Cline is still holding forth and work is progressing very satisfactorally.

I think I have been in Lima. I inspected a diesel engine mfg. co there once, I believe. Isn't Cooper Bessmer located there?

I'll bet those civilian clothes feel as comfortable as a fireplace now. The best of luck in your work and I hope your wife recovers rapidly.

The men send their regards and best wishes.

Very Sincerely,
Mr. McCall

124 N. 14th Street
Fort Pierce, Fla.
19 April, 1945

Dear Bob,

Have often wondered why there has been no reply to my last letter. Am afraid you have shipped out again. Sure hope this reaches you and that you can find time to drop me a note.

I'm still holding forth here but can see the end almost in sight. This joint is closing down in a few more weeks and there is very little possibility that I will be left here as part of a skeleton crew. Don't know what to expect except a change.

I haven't heard a word from the ship. Roger Frost had a letter from his brother who saw the 196 in Key West on her way across. He said she had been converted back into the old LCI (Wardroom taken out, etc.) and was Commanded by his former fourth officer. Just wonder if Dick has our old tub.

Gee, I sure could use some news from the old guys. Frost never seems to get any and neither do I. I suppose most of those who were in trainining with me at Little Creek are gone out.

I know now what you meant when you said that married life was the thing. It the only life for me. We have moved into town—have a nice little house—and even though the place isn't as elaborate we find it more convenient and very satisfactory.

Let me know where you are and give out with some news. Remember me to Pat.

As ever
Mac

UNITED STATES NAVY

(Lt. Charles A. McCall, USNR
124 N. 14th St.
Ft. Pierce, Fla.)

                                                17 May (1945)

Dear Mama,

I haven't heard from you in several days but hope that everything is O.K. I keep thinking every day that there will be some word from John. Hope we hear soon.

Alice and I are fine. She's getting fat as a pig and I'm beginning to gain. The weather is awfully hot and seems to be getting hotter.

We went down to Palm Beach last week-end and had a very good time. It was the first time I had been away since coming here.

Tom's marriage was a complete surprise to me. I had a letter or two from him recently but he hadn't mentioned a thing about getting married. I don't know the gal.

Is Sue's husband still home? Tell her to write us when she can.

When will the kids school be out? We're still looking for Ducky to come down when she can.

I would like some news of some of the boys if you have any—Tom Smith, Chas. Clark & the others. Where is Tom McCall now?

Guess I'll close here—let me hear from you soon.

                                                Love,
                                                Charles

(Mrs. Chas. A. McCall
124 N. 14th St.
Ft. Pierce, Fla.
May 24, 1945)

Wednesday

Dear Mother McCall,

I have waited such a long time to write you until I'm almost ashamed to write now. I hope you will forgive me and I'll try to do better in the future.

I hope you are all fine and enjoying some nice spring weather. It is really hot here now and I can see that I'm really going to miss the mts this summer, but as long as we can be together I won't complain. We are both fine and Charlie is looking better every day. He is gaining a little weight, but not quite as much as I am. I guess he just isn't the type to get fat because he eats well and things that should make him gain, but it doesn't seem to help any. I guess it doesn't matter just as long as he feels good and has his average weight. He is such a wonderful husband and we are so very happy. I just pray that I'll never have to be away from him because he is so much of my life. I don't see how I could ever make it without him. If he ever went away again I'd have to make the best of it but it sure would be hard.

We are hoping and praying everyday to hear that John is safe and on his way home. That is the one thing Charlie needs to really put his mind at ease. I can understand how all of you must feel and I do pray he'll be home soon. I feel sure he will and we want you to wire us as soon as you hear.

I'm awfully sorry we got mixed up on the birthday and I hope you were able to settle it O.K I wanted to get gifts for you, but I couldn't find what I thought you would like, so we decided to send money. I hope you bought something for yourself and if you didn't I'm going to spank you when we get home again. I sure wish you could have had flowers for Mothers Day, but I guess I waited a little late to get an order in for them. We certainly would like to have been with you and I hope that next Mothers Day finds all of us home to stay.

How are all three of my little boys? Give them a big hug for me and tell them I hope to see them before too long. Tell Duckie we still plan for her to visit us when school is out.

It's almost time to start supper, so I'd better stop for this time. Here's lots of love to all of you from both of us.

Your Children,
Alice & Charles

P.S. Tell Pop he doesn't have to worry about me being skinney any more.

(Lt. Charles A. McCall, USNR
124 N. 14th St.
Ft. Pierce, Fla.)

May 24, 1945

Dear Mama,

Alice just called and told me that your wire had come. It certainly is wonderful news. Hardly know how to express my feelings and I know you are overjoyed.

Guess John couldn't say just when he will get there. It shouldn't be very long, however, and please wire me when he arrives. He will probably come via Miami and if I could just find out when I could probably contact him but guess I can't.

Had a letter from Tom today. He is at Little Creek and expects to go out again before very long.

Hope you are all well. Everything is fine with us. Write soon.

Love,
Charles

May 24, 1945

Dear Mama,

Alice just called and told me that your wire had come. It certainly is wonderful news. Hardly know how to express my feelings and I know you are overjoyed.

Guess John couldn't say just when he will get there. It shouldn't be very long, however, and please wire me when he arrives. He will probably come via Miami and if I could find out when I could probably contact him but guess I can't.

Had a letter from Tom today. He is at Little Creek and expects to go out again before very long.

Hope you are all well. Everything is fine with us. Write soon

Love,
Charles

(Mrs. Chas. A. McCall
124 N. 14th St.
Ft. Pierce, Fla.
May 25, 1945)

Thursday

Dear Mother McCall,

Just got the wire about John a few minutes ago. I called Charles the minute it came and I think he was speechless. I expect him home at noon to get a look at the telegram. I know how happy this has made all of you and I wish we could be there to share the wonderful news together. I guess that doesn't matter much as long as we know he is safe and will be home soon. I am so happy for all of you and I'll bet you feel ten years younger. I know Charles will be like a new man because he has been worrying an awful lot about John. He didn't talk about it much, but I could tell what was on his mind.

I wrote you yesterday so this is just a note to tell you how happy and thankful I am for the good news.

Love to all
Alice

Thursday

Dear Mother McCall,
    Just got the wire
about John a few minutes
ago. I called Charles the
minute it came and I
think he was speechless.
I expect him home at
noon to get a look at
the telegram. I know
how happy this has
made all of you and
I wish we could be
there to share the
wonderful news together.
I guess that doesn't
matter much as long as
we know he is safe
and will be home soon.
I am so happy for all
of you and I'll bet

you feel ten years younger.
I know Charles will be
like a new man because
he has been worrying
an awful lot about John.
He didn't talk about it
much, but I could tell
what was on his mind.

I wrote you yesterday
so this is just a note
to tell you how happy
and thankful I am
for the good news.

Love to all
Alice

Coronado
May 25

Dear Mac:

I was certainly glad to receive your letter this morning. I am down here at this ATB on Bureau orders. Here's the story:

When we got home in January all of us old Officers were restless and anxious to get shore duty. We were in Boston at the time, having brought the Ship down from Portsmouth where it underwent 30 days availability. Turck, Kemler and myself took a train to Washington, met Lieverman on it, and went to the Bureau the next day. Bland and Dickenson were there, working away in the Amphib Section. We were all granted change of duty—Turck getting a Diesel job with Comfibtralant, Kembler going to Norfolk and Lieverman and myself being assigned out here.

They were very nice to us at the Bureau and granted our requests because we had enough sea duty and because Comfibtralant would not release us. (I had a negative answer on me from them to my request to a change of duty).

I have since met Bill Riley who I saw one night in Boston where he was undergoing treatments at the Chelsea hospital for a sore back caused when he fell down his deckhouse. Bill is here on Bureau orders as is John Watts, Lemmon from the 18 and Ed Dangler, and Bill Straight. All the old fellows, with the exception of Dick Jones went to Washington and all of them were given shore duty. However, I have my doubts as to how long this gravey train is going to last as work is folding around here and the base is much over complimented with Officers. Fortunately, some of the Full Lts who have been here for 17 and 20 months are being shipped out. Evidently, there is a limit to what politics can do!

I saw the 42 several times. They are here, undergoing training this week. Dick is CO, Al is Communications. They have two other officers: John May, a mustang is Engineer, and Alderson Propps, a big boy from WVa is Exec. (He is a jg. and Al stepped aside for him).

Verton was transferred last week and that leaves only Ralston as the last of the old gang. I take it he is pretty lonesome; but he is kept busy handling the Engine Room.

I do very little around here. I am in Officer Training Department bilited as an instructor. Imagine that! We instruct Ensigns who are about to be assigned to APAs and AKAs. Some of my 'courses' are the OOD in Port; the OOD Underway; Study Transport Doctrine. None of us know how long this duty is going to hold out. I don't think it can last much longer what with the way they are being shipped out.

I received a letter this morning from Lathrop, the first in months. He writes that work is slackening off from his station.

How are you and the Skipper. Give her my best regards. I know married life must be agreeing with you. As for me, I am still one and alone and I don't like it. But, I see no prospects before me.

I am thinking a lot about my postwar work. I can't seem to be able to decide in my own mind just what I want to do after it's over. I have never been as restless mentally in my life as I am now. The death of FDR was a hard blow for all of us.

I have been up to LA several times over weekends and about all I can say for those jaunts is that they were expensive as hell. People up there must think that money grows on the streets. They all seem to be living under a fog of glamor and unreality coming out of Hollywood. There is no question about the climate, it really is good. The temperature stays about the same—there is plenty of sun and cool breezes. But still, I like my seasons. When it is winter I want to know it and I want to enjoy springtime. Here, there is too much of the same thing.

I saw Ed Cogly the other day; he is being detached from his group and is leaving for Washington where he will enter the Supply Corps! He asked about you.

John Detweiler still has a group and his time here is short. Tom Gore and his staff are gone. Commander Talliferro I believe is still here.

I spend most of my nights here on the base, a twenty minute small boat ride from San Diego. I play the slot machines, see movies, write letters and get by long boring days and evenings. I realize that I have soft duty and I'm not going to be a hypocrite about admitting it. Next week the ball team comes back and that will be something to do at night. Pepper Martin is the manager.

I would like to hear all about you so write me a nice long letter soon.

Did your brother, who missing in action in Germany, get home safely? Let me know.

Best regards
Len

(Lt. Charles A. McCall, USNR
124 N. 14th St.
Ft. Pierce, Fla.)

5 June (1945)

Dear Mama,

Your letter came yesterday and was glad to hear everyone is well. We are fine but this heat is really something to contend with. Hope it don't get any hotter. They say the reason for the extreme heat is that it's so dry. This is ordinarily the rainy season here but we have had very little.

Well, John should be home most any day now. I sure will be glad. Helen writes that she plans to come down around the first of July so I think I'll ask for a short leave about that time. Chances aren't so good for my getting it but I can try. Sure would be good for us all to be home again.

You mentioned something about points. The little lady handles that end of it and I refuse to have anything to do with it. However, she says she is very short on "red points" (what ever that is) and would appreciate any you can send. She seems to be doing O.K., though—at least I'm eating good.

This has been a wonderful place for food since we've been here. We've had fresh tomatoes, cucumbers, beans, squash, lettuce, etc. ever since we came. And if I have that, you know, I'm happy. We've been having fresh corn now for a month or more. The only thing I've missed has been fresh butter. We have to use the oleo due to scarcity of points.

Write when you have time and here's hoping I see you around the first of July.

Always
Charles

July
1945

Charles
and
Alice

17 August 1945

Dear Mama,

When I got married I thought I was going to be able to put some of this letter writing off on the wife but she dreads it as bad as I.

We haven't heard from you in some time but hope everything is O.K. Everything is fine with us except that the weather is beginning to get pretty hot.

Alice's Dad is down with us for a few days. He came down with some guy from Brevard who drove a truck load of cattle down. He'll only be here a couple of days, I guess.

Looks like my job here is rapidly coming to an end. Present plans (confidentially) are to close the base up in a couple of months. Don't have any idea where I'll go from here.

Guess you are beginning to plant your garden. However, Mr. Pettit says you had quite a freeze recently.

I'd better get a little work done now. Write when you can and give my love to all.

Always,
Charles

P.S. When does Ducky want to come down?

Saturday Night
October 20, 1945

My Darling Wife,

Well, I finally made it! Things were fouled up right to the last but I reported aboard about one o'clock this afternoon.

I know the first question—and the answer isn't quite as good as it might be. The Commander seems to be a swell egg and he put his cards on the table right away. He has been stuck with a lot more ships—there's around forty now—they are all in very bad condition and he doesn't have an engineer. In all probability he will be taking them home soon and I have the job of getting them ready for the trip thrown right into my lap. He told me that if the ships don't head back within a couple of months or so he will release me and let me go back. He can't hold me more than three months.

That's the story in a nut shell, Sweetheart. And there's nothing I can do about it right now but go to work.

It all means roughly this—I probably won't get home until after the first of the year. I'll probably go back with the ships and get my release after we arrive. And it means I'm going to be the busiest man around for the next five weeks. Just as a sample—we are due to sail from here in four days and I have five or six ships with major breakdowns. The commander warned me that I probably wouldn't be sleeping much—and I can see where he is right. The assignment of more ships has knocked the group command idea in the head.

Darling, please try not to be too disappointed because it's really not nearly as bad as it might have been. And there is always the possibility that the ships will sail for home real soon.

I had a big stack of letters from you—and, Sweetheart, they were the most wonderful letters I ever had. After I read them I just about had to take off and hide some place. You are so wonderful my Darling, and so sweet. You make me by far the most happy man in the whole world—and the way I love you! It makes me so mad at times like this when I can't have you to hold close and tell you the things that are in my heart. Darling, if you ever let me leave you again I'll just pass away. I've just got to get back to you before long.

The radio is playing "Dream." Seem like they are just trying to rub it in.

At least, I'm glad to have a post to hang my hat on. Ordinarilly, I think I would like this assignment fairly well. The officers I'll be working with seem to be very nice guys and I've got a job with a challenge to some real work. I'll tell you more about that as time goes on.

A stewart has just come in to help me unpack so I'll have to get busy. I'd better turn early because tomorrow looks like a hard day—but I promise to take off long enough to write a long letter telling you more about me. Until then, goodnight to the most wonderful wife in the world. I love my Bedie*

Always
your Charlie

*Grandma Alice had been called "Bedie" by her family since infancy. When her older brother, Uncle Bruce, tried to say "baby", it came out "Bedie." Unfortunately, it stuck for life; a curse of the South!

Saturday Night
October 20, 1945

My Darling Wife,

Well, I finally made it! Things were fouled up right to the last but I reported aboard about one o'clock this afternoon.

I know the first question - and the answer isn't quite as good as it might be. The commander seems to be a swell egg and he put his cards on the table right away. He has been stuck with a lot more ships - there's around forty now - they are all in very bad condition and he doesn't have an engineer. In all probability he will be taking them home soon and I have the job of getting them ready for the trip thrown right into my lap. He told me that if the ships don't head back within a couple of months or so, he will release me and let me go back. He can't hold me more than three months.

CHAPTER TWELVE

New Life Begins

Grandpa Charlie spent the last quarter of 1945 in Japan repairing ships of the United States Naval fleet for their return home. When he left for the Pacific in October, Grandma Alice went home to North Carolina and lived with her parents for the remainder of the year. After Grandpa Charlie's return, they stayed in Brevard until early March 1946, when he got job with the state unemployment commission in Wadesboro, N.C. Just two months later, Grandpa Charlie, still a member of the Naval Reserve, got a civilian job as a Mathematician and Ordinance Engineer with the Army Field Forces No.1 at Fort Bragg, N.C. (This was later to become the U.S. Army Artillery Board and relocate to Oklahoma.) In May, 1946, he and Grandma Alice moved to Fayetteville, N.C., the sister city of the Ft. Bragg Army Base. Still in North Carolina but a long way from home, they continued to write letters to Grandma Delphie telling of the new life they were making together in post WWII America. The letters that remain begin in March 1946, continue on through 1947, the year of my and many other "Baby Boomers" birth, and end with just two letters from 1948. And so we begin the final chapter of our journey.

Alice & Charles McCall

27 West Ave.
Wadesboro, N.C.
(March 8, 1946)

Dear Mama,

Guess you're having a hard time keeping track of your boy these days. I really hated to run off without seeing any of you but it was a case of necessity. I was in Brevard at three in the afternoon when I agreed to accept this job. The man called Raleigh and they wanted me there the next morning at nine. I had to go down to the school house, put my records in order there, pack up and get started. We left Brevard about eight and arrived in Raleigh at five the next morning. I went to school there Thursday, Friday and Saturday.

Saturday afternoon we drove down to La Grange and visited a while with Uncle Loon. They sure were surprised to see us and I hardly knew them—it had been so long. We had a nice visit and exchanged a lot of news.

We came down here Sunday and I started to work Monday morning. I am an interviewer for the North Carolina Unemployment Compensation Commission. I certainly do like the work and I'm really busy. I usually have a line of fifty or more in front of my office all day long. The days sure pass in a hurry.

Alice got out and found an apartment Monday afternoon and we moved right in. It's a pretty nice place and we are much happier than we were in Brevard. It sure is fine to have a place to cook and feel at home again.

We had planned to come back home this week-end to get some more of our things but decided to put if off a week. If nothing happens, we'll see you then. Give everyone our love and write to us.

Lots of love,
Charles

Mrs. Chas. A. McCall
27 West Ave.
Wadesboro, N.C.
(March 21, 1946)

Wednesday, P.M.

Dear Mama,

I guess you'll really be surprised getting a letter from me. It's been so long since I wrote you, but now that we're settled maybe I'll do better. I hope so anyway.

We made the trip back with no trouble except for some rain and fog. That, of course, slowed us down, but we got here O.K.

Sure was good to see all of you again and I wish we could have spent more time with you. Next time I hope we won't have so much to do, so we can see more of you.

Thanks so much for the things you gave us. I'm going to have some of the beans tonight and try to make some good cornbread to go with them. That's something Charles always likes.

Mama, I know there is no use to tell you how wonderful your son and my husband is, because you already know. I just like to tell you how happy I am to have someone like him. I only hope I can always give him the happiness he deserves and be a wife he will always be proud of. I guess that sounds a little silly to you, but he is so wonderful and I'm so proud of him. I just have to tell you the way I feel.

I hope you are all feeling fine. We are both feeling good and getting plenty of rest. I do hope Charles can gain some weight now that we're settled for awhile.

Take care of yourself and let us hear from you soon. Lots of love to all of you.

Alice & Charles

P.S. I guess you discovered we forgot our clock. Maybe we can think of it next time we come up. I think we can make out alright without until then.

Bye, Bye-

Alice & Charles McCall

27 West Ave.
Wadesboro, N.C.
Sunday
Afternoon
7 April 1946

Dear Mama,

It sure is a beautiful day down here. Spring has really come—the trees are green, flowers are blooming and the birds are singing. It's a fine afternoon to be out but Alice isn't feeling very well so we're staying in and I'm trying to catch up with a few letters.

We missed church this morning—the first time since we've been here. I hate to miss it because the pastor, I think, is about the best preacher I have ever heard. He visits us right often and he and I played golf yesterday.

I sure am sorry for Alice when these periods come around for her. She suffers something awful and tries to keep me from knowing just how bad it does hurt. Doctors have told her that having a baby is the only thing that will help and we hope to take care of that before very long. Just as soon, in fact, as we can settle down with a little permanency.

I have not settled down with this job for good. It's a good place to be to find a good place, though. We get job openings from all over the country and I send in several applications every week. I'm anxious to find something good and get really settled down—build a house, etc.

The clock came through in good shape but I almost lost my knife. I didn't see it in the box and it fell out just before I dumped the box in the garbage can.

If nothing happens, we will be up for the Easter week-end. I have to go to Charlotte on Saturday to take and examination and if it doesn't take too long, we might drive up there then but it's doubtful.

How is everyone getting along? School will be out soon and you'll have the boys with you—guess there'll be plenty for them to do. I'm planting me a garden down here so I'm going to be pretty busy too.

Write to us and give everyone our regards.

"Oodles" of love
Charles

Mrs. Chas. A. McCall
27 West Ave.
Wadesboro, N.C.

(April 15, 1946)

Monday Afternoon

Dearest Mama,

Just a few lines to let you know we will see you this week-end. I'm hoping we will be able to spend more time with you than we did the last time. Charles has Mon. off, so we'll be able to stay longer. He has his heart set on doing some fishing, and I hope he will be able to.

How is everything with all of you? We are both fine and have nothing to complain about. I guess that's pretty good. Tell Pop we're coming up to get something good to eat this week-end, so he better be prepared. I'll have to tell you about our experience dressing a chicken when I see you. You'll really get a good laugh.

We went to Charlotte Sat. and spent the day. Charles had to take an Exam. up there, so we just made a day of it. The Exam. he took was supposed to be 4 hrs. long, and he finished it in 45 minutes. We don't know how he made out yet, but I'm sure he done alright.

We had a long letter from Helen one day last week. They seem to be a little upset about Roy's job. I guess she wrote you about it. I sure hope it works out alright for them.

Since there isn't much to write about I'll stop for now. We'll see you this week-end and have some coffee while we talk. Lots of love to all.

Alice & Charles

308 Person St.
Fayetteville, N.C.
May 12, 1946
(postcard)

Dear Mama,

We arrived safely and have a room at above address. Housing situation don't look as bad as it might be.

Happy Mother's Day. Will write more soon

Charles

F-15—First Baptist Church,
Fayetteville, N. C.

5B-H76

308 Pine St.
Fayetteville, N.C.

Dear Mama,
        We arrived
safely and have a
room at above address.
Housing situation don't
look as bad as it
might be.
        Happy Mother's day.
Will write more soon
                Charles

CAROLINA NEWS CO., FAYETTEVILLE, N. C.

GENUINE CURTEICH-CHICAGO "C.T. ART-COLORTONE" POST CARD (REG. U.S. PAT. OFF.)

POST CARD

Mrs. Clyde L. M. Call
Lake Toxaway, N.C.

Lake Toxaway, NC
June 24, 1946)

Mrs. Charles A. McCall
520 Elm St.
Fayetteville, N.C.

Mon. Morning

Dear Alice,

I am wondering if you have found a place to live and how you and Charles a feeling. Guess its hot down there now. Its not been so cool here the past week. The mercury was standing at 87 at bed time one night last week. Any way it seems to agree with gardens. We have very fine irish potatoes, beans and a few other things. We had a nice cooling shower yesterday after noon.

I have been intending to answer your letter for some time and just had been busy. With the children around every day I most always have three meals to prepare and with a hundred and one other things to do I do not have too much leasure time. So please have that in mind and don't think *too* hard.

Charles said in his last letter he was liking his work. I am glad he does.—

Monday morning again and here I am trying to write. I started this letter last Monday and failed to remember the new address. It was on the package you sent daddy. The wrapper has been misplaced and for this cause I'll have to send it to the first address hoping it will be forwarded to you. I have been hoping to hear from you all all week.

I am just wondering if you all are still planning to come up the 4th and if you would like to have a *picnic dinner (say out the Bohaney road) or some place. (If you have not already planned something else) I have some nice friers I could fix and we could fix dinner with out too much trouble. We usually have a picnic dinner and the kids always look forward to it. So think about it and if you decide to, write or just come anyway.

We are all just still at the same old routine of duties daddy is still painting. I guess he will until school starts.

Chester and Fanny came yesterday and stayed awhile—they seem just like always. They said James is going to law school and that they plan to go back to their farm any time if Chester is laid off his job at Charlstar.

Well I guess I started off to answer Alice letter and ended up writing to you both, but write soon and come up the 4th if you can.

Love as ever
Mama

* I fondly remember Grandma Delphi's picnics—fried chicken, biscuits, potato salad, deviled eggs, green beans, fresh tomatoes & cucumbers, coconut cake—yummmm!! These were summer feast rituals she began with her children and continued as they would say in the mountains, "with all us cousins."

Mon. Morning

Dear Alice.
    I am wondering if you have
found a place to live and how you and
Charles a feeling. Guess its hot down
there now. its not been so cool here the past
week. the mercury was standing at 87 at
bed time one night last week. any way
it seems to agree with gardens. we have
very fine irish potatoes beans and a few
other things. we had a nice cooling shower
yesterday after noon.
    I have been intending to answer
your letter for some time and just had
been busy. with the children around every
day I most always have three meals to
prepare and with a hundred and one
other things to do I do not have too
much leasure time. So please have that
in mind and don't think too hard.
    Charles said in his last letter
he was liking his work. I am glad
he does. —
    Monday Morning again and

(520 Elm St.
Fayetteville, N.C.
June 26, 1946)

Tuesday

Dear Mama,

It has been two weeks since I have heard from you and I wonder if anything is wrong. It may be that our mail is mixed up somewhere but you should have our address now. I hope you are well and that everyone is O.K.

We are fine—working hard and staying at home. Alice went to work yesterday—she has a job with a finance company down town. I wasn't too well pleased to see her start work but the little two-room apartment wasn't enough to keep her busy during the day and she got awfully lonesome. She has a good job and thinks she will like it O.K.

We still haven't fully decided whether or not to go home for the fourth. I'll have from Wednesday afternoon until Monday off from work and I suppose Alice could get off. My car isn't in shape to drive that far and I'm having trouble finding parts to get it fixed. If I don't, we would have to go by bus and I'm afraid they will be awfully crowded about that time. We'll make up our mind soon and let you know whether or not to expect us.

If we do get home, I would like for us to take off on a picnic one day. That shouldn't be hard to arrange.

We haven't seen many people down here that we know so far—only three or four. I keep thinking that I will run into some soldiers from around there but I suppose most all of them are out of the Army by now.

Mrs. Pettit wrote us that Ford Owen had been seriously sick from food poisoning. Is he any better—

What are the boys doing mostly? When we finally get a place to live, I want some of them to come down to see us for a while—that is if I find something before school starts again.

Right now I am about to buy a new house. It's one of those being built by the Veterans housing outfit and sells for about three prices. But for a very reasonable down payment I can finish paying for it by monthly payments which would be less than what I pay for rent on the little place we have now. So I figure I couldn't loose much on the deal under any circumstances. The only reason I am hesitating now is the problem of furniture. After looking around and figuring with several stores in town I'm astounded. Everything is completely beyond reason. If I saw any hope for things to become more reasonable during the next year or so I would wait—but I don't see much hope of that.

I'd better do a little work now. Do write often and when you don't have time to write or don't feel like it, ask one of the kids to drop us a line. We think about you all the time and sure miss hearing from you.

Love to all
Charles

(July 15, 1946)

520 Elm St.
Fayetteville
Sunday Afternoon

Dear Mama,

I'm actually ashamed of the way I have let you down by not writing more than I have during the past several days. For some reason or other I just can't seem to get a letter started any more.

It's so terribly hot here now that I don't feel like doing much of anything. We got up about eight this morning and it was already so hot we were sweating. For that reason we didn't go to church and I never feel good about missing. Guess we shouldn't let hot weather keep us away but I just don't feel like getting dressed on a day like this.

Ma Pettit called this morning and told us about John's new heir. I'm happy for them and terribly jealous. He's getting way ahead of me—but I'm trying.

Did I tell you about my raise? Starting on the first of July I was raised $500 a year. That puts me up to $350 a month and with Alice making almost half that much it seems that we should be well off—but it sure gets away from you. I'm saving all I possibly can in hope that we'll find a good deal in a house pretty soon. I sure am anxious to get a place of my own.

Have you heard from Helen lately? She must be peeved at us or something. I have written her twice and Alice once since we heard from her. Maybe she is just awfully busy. When we last heard from her she talked like they planned to come back to Franklin to live.

How is Sue and her family. Reckon they never write anyone.

We are still living in our little two room apartment. We don't like it but we are sure having a hard time finding anything else. I found a five room place yesterday and for $100 a month—can't quite see that.

Write soon and take care of yourself. We love you.

Always,
Charles

Office of Price Administration

IN REPLY REFER TO:

Cincinnati, O
July 24 (1946
830 Cleveland Ave
Cincinnati, 29,O.)

Dear Mac:

As you can see by this letterhead I am back again with the government. I have been working for OPA since the first of June. I am in the Information Office, part of the District Office which is located in Cincy and services the southern half of Ohio. Frankly, things have been very quiet and inactive the past two or three weeks, for obvious reasons, I think. Sometimes I think I am back on the 42, especially when I go downstairs for Coffee and catch up on my reading.

I heard from Columbia and the answer was negative. They have over 500 applicants for the Journalism School and only 60 openings. I have decided to stay out of school, at least for the present and see what I can do for myself on the outside. Your suggestion about North Carolina for Journalism was a good one, I have heard that they have an excellent school down there. As a matter of fact one of the leading Professors in the School of Journalism (I can't recall his name) played a leading part in the Des Moines convention of the American Veterans Committee. So he is a liberal. We have a chapter here and have close to 150 members. Most of them are Drs., lawyers, and Vets with a decided professional flavor. The program appeals more to men in good financial condition who want to consider themselves liberals. I would much prefer to see the average type guy, who, I believe goes more for the Legion type of organization. I am an old member of the Cincinnati Chapter AVC am chairman of the Minorities Committee and in charge of a raffle (two cases of whiskey the purpose of which is to equip our treasury with greenbacks). I am sure that if you were here you would buy some tickets.

I see where a group of leading Americans, including your friend Frank Graham have gone on record in favor of a labor-management conference now to meet and overcome the coming price-wage crises which is expected this fall or the first of the year due to rapidly rising prices and the virtual junking of OPA controls. Thanks, in large part, to the current picture must rest with 'Cincinnati's own' Bob Taft, who is less popular around here than he is in the farm areas of the state. I read Madam Sun's statement with interest and concern. If Chaing can only offer the Chinese peasants a choice between the rule of the Koumintang or Civil War I don't think he is going to get very far, even if he does have sizable quantities of US equiptment. He must have a real democratic program that will answer some of the problems that face the hungry Chinese. China is the one place in all the world where American and Russian interests meet, and could clash and a large scale Civil War there would make real and dangerous, a Madam Sun pointed out, the possibilities of the fires spreading dangerously.

Remember the big fellow who was Bos'n on the 189? He's a policeman here in town. He used to kid me a lot overseas and say he would pull me in when he got me back to Cincinnati. A couple of months ago I was drinking beer on the hill and who walks in on his 'beat' but the Chief. As usual, I can't remember his name but, I'm sure you remember him: tall, husky, good looking, dark hair, and exceptionally friendly.

A very dear friend of mine, Dr. George Hedger, Professor of History retired this year after 25 years at the University and is now in Wyoming on his way to the west coast where he will live in a small house with a small acerage with his wife and son. That man was a strong influence in my life: an outstanding man of kindly bent, liberal and fair in everything he did, a great scholar. He edited and complied a History of Civilization that is used in many universities. His colleague in the Department organized a dinner in his honor last May and not enough of his sincere friends were there and there were far too many platitudes thrown out. Isn't it hard to properly evaluate a man in his presence? At the affair for Dr. Hedger there were naturally present the top officials of the University and by and large they did not appreciate some of the more courageous acts of his career, O in behalf of the Civil Liberties Union, for example, and it seemed to me that only those who really appreciated what Dr. Hedger stands for should have been invited. Perhaps the others learned something worthwhile attending.

My mother is now visiting my sister in Durham and it is a good thing for her to get away from town. My niece is a joy to her and certainly helps give her mother a new lease on life.

I am glad you have a good job and can use your knowledge of math to good advantage. Regards to the little women and the best of luck to you

write often

as ever

Len

(Lake Toxaway, NC
July 8, 1946)

Mon July 8

Dear Charles

I received your letter last week but did not answer thinking you would come up for the week end. We had a nice time and the children liked our dinner and trip fine. We went up to Berlins lake. I fixed dinner for all of us thinking maybe you and Alice would come. We missed you all so much. Hope it won't be long till you will be coming again.

How are you both? Is Alice feeling good? Are you doing alright? I think about you all so much.

The children are attending a Bible school it began last Monday and will last all this week. Alconia McCall is teaching. They seem very much interested and don't want to miss any.

We went over last Sunday and stayed awhile with Grandma and Grandpa. They seem to be getting along about as well as usual. Grandma is very feeble Ford has got over his sick spell and they all seem to be fine.

I think it is nearly time for Doris' baby to come. I kindly dread keeping Joe for berries are beginning to ripen and I'll have so much to do. I am feeling much better than when you were here but still it will be such a busy time.

You know its not long till your birthday. Its hard for me to realize you are a man but I guess you really are. I am sure Alice and me thinks that Transylvania has never produced a finer one, that's the way I feel.

I'll have to stop now its mail time daddy is off to-day and I'll have to have dinner when the kids get back.

Bushels of love
Mama

Dear Son,

    Just a word to go along with mama's letter. I haven't written a letter to anyone in so long that I've forgotten the art of it. I've been working so hard for the last month that my thinking apparatus has become dormant and my physical propensities are over developed. So you can see a fellow geared up like that will not do much at writing as it takes little muscle and some brains.

    We missed you children very much in the fried chicken contest the Fourth. You being absent the honors of the day went to the winner, Jerry.

    We are all well at this time—really doing better in that line than we were when you were here last.

                                      Best Wishes
                                      Daddy Mc

Dear Son, just a word to go
along with mama's letter. I haven't
written a letter to anyone in so
long that I've forgotten the art of it.
I've been working so hard for the
last month that my thinking apparatus
has become dormant and my
physical propensities are over
developed. So you can see
a fellow geared up like that
will not do much at writing as
it takes little muscle and
some brains.

We missed you children
very much in the fried chicken
contest the Fourth. You being absent
the honors of the day went to the
winner, Jerry.

We are all well at this
time. really doing better in
that line than we were
when you were here last.

Best Wishes
Daddy Mc

(721 A. McGilvary St.
Fayetteville, N.C.)

August 22 (1946)

Dear Mama,

I'm beginning to wonder what has happened up there—it's been weeks since I have heard from you. I hope that "no news is good news" will hold true in this case.

We are getting along O.K.—still trying to get our house furnished and fixed up. It's looking better all the time.

We were down town last Saturday buying groceries and who should we run into but Uncle Loon. He is living about eight miles out of Fayetteville and we went to see them Sunday afternoon. He has a nice school out there but sure is having trouble trying to hire teachers.

Alice hasn't been feeling so well lately. I think she has been working too hard and I haven't been able to slow her down. I'm going to take her to a Doctor tomorrow and get her straightened out.

I guess Summer is about over up there. It's still pretty hot here but not as bad as it was a month ago.

Try to find time to write us now and then. We like to hear from you.

Love always,
Charles

(721 A. McGilvary St.
Fayetteville, N.C.
(Sep 19, 1946)

Monday

Dear Mama,

A week is a short vacation but even with that it takes some time to get back into the groove. I know I should have written before now but for one reason or another I have neglected doing do.

We left Brevard early Sunday morning and had a slow but safe trip back. Much to my surprise and relief, the old car gave us no trouble at all.

We didn't get around as much while we were there as we planned to. I wanted to get over to see Grandpa Owen's Folks and a lot of other people—guess a week is just too short. Nevertheless, we enjoyed ourselves and I came back to work with a nice rested feeling.

I meant to tell you before I left—Go ahead and do what you think is best about the heifer. I wish I had some place to keep her but I haven't. Perhaps the next time you can breed the cow to some good stock again and save me the calf.

I have been reading about the big plane crash up there but can't figure out just where it was. Sounds like it might have been up around Shoal Creek.

Guess you're anxiously awaiting Helen's visit. Sure hope we can arrange some way to her.

Give everyone out love and write often

Always
Charles

(721 A. McGilvary St.
Fayetteville, N.C.)

Thursday A.M.
January 23, 1947

Dear Mama,

I hope getting a letter from me won't be too much of a surprise for you. I have had good intentions for a long time, so this morning I decided to do something about it.

Sure hope you are all feeling fine these days. I guess the kids are all over the mumps and back in school. Tell them they'd better be well next time I come home, so I won't have to stay away. We are both fine and I'm getting fatter every day. I wonder why? My Dr. says I'm doing fine and my weight is what it should be. Charlie thought I was gaining too much, but the Dr. says not. So far everything is O.K. and I hope it continues to be.

Charlie is still planning to go on the cruise, but he hasn't heard anymore from the Navy. They will probably wait until the last minute to let him know.

Mama, I want to thank you again for the things you gave us. I'm enjoying my apron so much, and it was so nice of you to make it for me.

We have been trying all week to get a couple of birthday gifts on the way to Daddy Mac & Joe Ben, and we still haven't done it. Tell them they should get something soon. We got all mixed up on dates again, and I'm awfully sorry about it. I should keep a list of our birthday dates, so we wouldn't get behind.

How are you feeling? I had such a short talk with you last time I didn't have much of a chance to ask you anything. I hope you are feeling good and not working too hard.

Guess I'd better let this be all for now as I have some work to do.

Give our love to all and write us real soon.

Love
Alice

(721 A. McGilvary St.
Fayetteville, N.C.)

Sunday Night
February 2 (1947)

Dear Mama,

Sure was glad to get your letter. Seems that I would write you more often since I enjoy hearing from you so much. It's just so hard to get started.

We missed church this morning. One of the neighbors had to go out of town to a funeral and we kept their little girl for them.

I'm leaving here Friday for my cruise. We haven't decided for sure yet what Alice will do. She wants to go home but I won't agree to it until she gets her doctor's permission. She's going to ask him tomorrow. If she doesn't go, her mother is coming down to stay with her. I would like for her to go home if it will be O.K.

We're having a time getting some uniforms together. I had most of them converted and now I'm having to get them reconverted.

I hope the kids got over their mumps O.K. Suppose they did since you didn't mention it.

Everything is O.K. with us. We're sure having some beautiful weather—just like Spring.

Give everyone our love and write to us.

Love,
Charles

Sunday Night
February 2

Dear Mama,

Sure was glad to get your letter. Seems that I would write you more often since I enjoy hearing from you so much. It's just so hard to get started.

We missed church this morning. One of the neighbors had to go out of town to a funeral and we kept their little girl for them.

I'm leaving here Friday for my cruise. We haven't decided for sure yet what Alice will do. She wants to go home but I won't agree to it until she gets her doctor's permission. She's going to ask him tomorrow. If she doesn't go, her mother is coming down to stay with her. I would like for her to go home if it will be o.k.

We're having a time getting some uniforms together. I had most of them converted and now I'm having to get them reconverted.

I hope the kids got over their mumps ok. Suppose they did since you didn't mention it.

Everything is ok with us. We're sure having some beautiful weather - just like Spring.

Give everyone our love and write to us.

Love,
Charles

(Fort Bragg, N.C.
Feb 7, 1947)

Friday

Dear Mama,

I'm getting ready to leave so this is just a note.

Alice left this morning on the bus. Her mother is meeting her in Charlotte and they will spend the night with an uncle there. I hesitated to let her go but the Doctor told her if she would stop over for a night it would be O.K. Suppose she will get to Brevard tomorrow or Sunday and will be seeing you.

I'm leaving for Charleston this afternoon and will be back two weeks from Sunday. Guess I picked a good time because it sure is cold here now.

Hope everyone is well—love to all

Charles

1 A. McGilvary St.
Fayetteville, N.C.)

Thursday
(March, 1947)

Dear Mama,

Seems that you and I are both are getting worse when it comes to writing letters. I usually figure that as long as I don't hear from you, everything is O.K. so I don't let it bother me too much. Hope you figure it the same way.

Things are going as good as can be expected with us. Alice's trip didn't seem to bother her a all—for which I am thankful. Her energy is pretty low now but the Doc says that is normal and I suppose I shouldn't expect her to be as full of life as she ordinarily is. She has less than two months to go now.

We went down town Saturday and bought the things for the baby's room. I just finished painting it and we're having lots of fun getting it all fixed up. We're just about ready now and I am praying everything will go well. We can hardly wait.

There seems to be a slight epidemic of flu around here now. We are staying in pretty close in an attempt to avoid it—sure hope we can.

Aunt Viola was by to see us one night last week and we saw Uncle Loon in town Saturday. They are getting along fine—getting ready to build them a house down near Aunt Viola's folks. Her mother, who is an invalid, is pretty sick and may not live much longer.

I hear you've had plenty of snow up there the past few weeks. Sure wish I could have seen some of it. *I don't believe I will ever grow up when it comes to getting a thrill out of seeing it snow. We had just a wee bit down here last Sunday but none of it stuck to the ground.

Lots of things have been happening up there since I saw you—Mack Robinson's suicide, Earl Reid's murder, etc. I need to catch up on all the gossip.

Hope you are feeling better now than when Alice was there. Maybe we'll have some Spring weather soon that will be good for you—but don't work too hard. Give everyone our love and write soon

Always
Your Charles

* I remember, after we moved to Oklahoma where it snowed very seldom back then, Daddy getting us up and being so excited when it snowed. We'd make a snowman, snow angels and best of all snow cream which was so delicious I can still almost taste it.

Tuesday, April 22
(1947)

Dear Mama,

I'm so busy now that it is difficult to find time to write a letter. Everything is fine, however, so I hope you don't worry about us.

It is less than two weeks now until the big event—in fact, the doctor says it may come most any day. I think we are ready. Mrs. Pettit is coming down on the first if we don't notify her sooner. I'm glad she is coming for Alice's sake. The doctor says that Alice is doing nicely. He has had her on a diet for a couple of months because she started gaining too much weight. She doesn't sleep too well these nights and is a little uncomfortable but I suppose that is to be expected. I can't tell you anything about that part of it, can I?

I was a little afraid that you were going to crawfish on me about coming down but you still haven't convinced me. They can get along without you for a few days even if they have to live with the neighbors. I had hoped to have an automobile by this Summer so that I would be able to go up and get you (and I may) but I don't think you would mind the trip by bus too much. Some of this hot weather and sunshine down here would be good for you.

Uncle Loon and the folks were up to see us Sunday afternoon. He is well now and they are getting along O.K. Aunt Viola always brings us butter, a cake, or something and we are glad to see them come. Uncle Loon couldn't get along if he didn't see "Alice" once in a while. He is undecided whether he wants to remain here for another year. He doesn't like the school very well and, of course, has all kinds of offers to go other places. But, like all of us, he hates to move so much. Vance is still in Japan. Uncle Loon wants to come up there soon as school is out and spend several weeks but I doubt he'll do it. He says he would build him a cottage up there if he wasn't afraid Uncle Homer's boys would tear it down. Uncle Till did a good job of indoctrinating him on those boys.

I haven't heard from Helen in months. I guess it's my fault because I just can't write any more, it seems. And of course, John and Sue never write—probably my fault too. Let me know how they are getting along. Do Helen and Roy plan to come down this Summer?

It seems that the cost of living continues to rise down here instead of coming down. Everybody has gone money-crazy and I hate to think about where it is going to take us. President Truman gave out some sound advice the other day but, of course, no one is paying any attention to it. I'm on a buyers strike myself—I refuse to buy anything but bare necessities until things get a little better.

Have you started your garden yet. They sure are going to be a big help this Summer and I wish I had a place for one.

Give our regards to everyone and write to us.

Love
Charles

(121 A McGilvary St.
Fayetteville, N.C.)

Thursday, February 12
(1948)

Dear Mama,

This certainly is a rough day here. We had a five-inch snow a couple of days ago and it's pouring down the rain today making a sloppy mess. This is the only time that snows are disagreeable to me—I sure get a kick out of them.

I'm sorry that I have waited so long to write—I've really been busy for a couple of weeks. I have two tests going on today but I have some good men in charge so I'm going to take it easy. I need some rest.

Uncle Loon came by Sunday and told me about his trip. It was rough going for them. I had called Uncle Marvin the night before they left from there to get word to them that Aunt Viola had gotten fuel oil, there would be no school for a few days, and for them not to hurry back. However, Uncle Marvin was at work, Aunt Ruby answered the phone and consequently they didn't get the word. They were brave (or foolish) to start out when they did. Uncle Loon tickled me good. He said he would have stayed a few days but Vance was restless and wanted to start back. I can well imagine who the restless one was.

I'm worried a little about fuel oil myself for the first time. My extra tank is empty and I have about enough to last three or four days. If the roads clear up during that time, however, I'll probably get some. Most of it comes into this place by truck. I'm not worried about freezing since we can heat a couple of rooms with our gas range if it comes to that—but that's expensive. But fuel oil isn't cheap—my bills for the past three months have averaged twenty dollars a month.

You should see your grand daughter. She has a mouth full of teeth and can take several steps. She doesn't make much effort to talk though. I tell Alice it's because she gets everything she wants without it. She says a few little things when she's in the mood—like "mama", "bye-bye", etc. She had an appointment with her doctor today but it is so rough that we decided not to take her out. He hasn't seen her now in about two months.

Are schools running there? All rural schools here are closed indefinitely. I think Uncle Loon has taught a half day since he came back.

It seems that prices are taking a drop—and none too soon. It would please me to see the bottom fall out for a while. Everything was getting unreasonable.

I'm going to the Navy for two weeks soon. Alice wants to go home while I'm away so I'm waiting until the weather gets a little warmer.

Write soon and take care of yourself.

Love Always,
Charles

May 17, 1948

Dear Mama,

At this stage of the game, I'm almost too ashamed of myself to begin a letter. I couldn't possibly forget such a wonderful mother on the double occasion of Mother's day and your birthday. Getting back home and setting things straight there and getting caught up on the job has had me jumping. If you will forgive me, I'll make it right shortly.

On top of everything else, I have had one of these terrible Summer colds for the past week. I spent the whole week-end in bed and feel much better now. Alice has a touch of her old kidney trouble and feels pretty low. We worry about trips being tough on Pat but she seems to be able to take more than we can. She's doing fine.

I hope you folks are well and happy. I know Ducky & the boys are thrilled over school ending pretty soon.

I have no news of interest. We spent last Sunday out at Uncle Loon's. We had a good time and a wonderful dinner but poor little Pat had a hectic day. Cubby and Mary Ida won't leave her alone for a minute. Vance comes to see us two or three times a week.

Tell Jerry that I'm sending him a bus ticket when school is out. I want all of you to come sometime during the Summer. Joe Ben can come with you and Ducky and Dan later. Try to get Daddy to plan a trip—he will enjoy looking around.

Write us soon if it's just a card. Alice and Pat send their love.

Always
Charles

May 17, 1948

Dear Mama,

At this stage of the game, I'm almost too ashamed of myself to begin a letter. I couldn't possibly forget such a wonderful mother on the double occasion of mothers day and your birthday. Getting back home and setting things straight there and getting caught up on the job has had me jumping. If you will forgive me, I'll make it right shortly.

On top of everything else, I have had one of these terrible summer colds for the past week. I spent the whole week-end in bed and feel much better now. Alice has a touch of her old kidney trouble and feels pretty low. We worry about trips being tough on Pat but she seems to be able to take more than we can. She's doing fine.

I hope you folks are all well and happy. I know Ducky & the boys are thrilled over school ending pretty soon.

I have no news of interest. We spent last Sunday out at Uncle Loon's. We had a good time and a wonderful dinner but poor little Pat had a hectic day. Cubby and Mary Ida won't leave her alone for a minute. Vance comes to see us two or three times a week.

Tell Jerry that I'm sending him a bus ticket when school is out. I want all of you to come sometime during the summer. Joe Ben can come with you and Ducky and Dan later. Try to get Daddy to plan a trip - he will enjoy looking around.

Write us soon if it's just a card. Alice and Pat send their love.

always
Charles

EPILOGUE

G randma Delphie's trunk contained a sprinkling of letters and postcards after 1948, through the remaining decades of Grandpa Charlie's life; but these were letters from a new era. His focus had shifted from the family in which he grew up to his and Grandma Alice's own growing family. In August 1954, immediately after my baby brother, Allen, was born, came the momentous move to Oklahoma. By this time the telephone had become the main avenue of communication for most folks, although, I don't remember Grandma McCall having one for quite a while. Since the letters began in the fall of 1937, when Grandpa Charlie went off to college, and I have ended with the letters of May, 1948, this book holds ten years of literary windows into his soul.

So, what have we learned about Charles Allen McCall? We know he was highly intelligent, and unusually so, being accomplished in both language and mathematics. He was a deep thinker, an enthusiastic student of life and the world. He was a leader in his family, college and the Navy; he was admired and respected by many folks. He had a strong spiritual longing and possessed the soul of a poet. He had a primal connection to the earth and was most at home when outdoors, surrounded by natural beauty. He loved his family, cared very much about their welfare, longed for their company and enjoyed giving them gifts, whether it be postcards from around the world, a new coat, or money for a cow. He loved his mother with a love he could not express in words, and he loved and respected his father. He was strong and handsome and brave; he was a decorated war hero. He was a cultured, Renaissance man who loved books, history, music, food and beauty. He was fun and funny, with an earthy sense of humor. He was keenly interested in current affairs and politics, a Democrat and a liberal. He treasured his many close friends and enjoyed their company immensely. He had a natural ease of expression with the written word. Most of all he was full of life and love and the promise of tomorrow.

Charles Allen McCall and Alice Pettit McCall had four children, Eleanor Patricia, Charles Allen, Jr., John David and Alice Anne. As the first born, I have the longest memories of my Father. During my early years he would take me to "town" every Saturday morning to see the parrot in the pet shop and hear it say "Polly Want a Cracker", and then for cherry sodas at the old fashioned drug store next door. To this day, if I want to feel close to my Daddy, I treat myself to a cherry soda. Sometimes on these outings he would buy me something. I remember one Easter season he bought me a plush baby blue coat and a bunny dyed the same color. You could dye bunnies and chicks back then, but the poor little thing didn't last long. I think Grandpa Charlie put him out of his misery, although he never told me he did. On Saturday or Sunday afternoons he would take me for long walks in the woods, delighting in pointing out to me all the flora and fauna. My Daddy had a big easy chair by our large console radio; after supper I would crawl up in his lap and we would listen to *Jack Benny* and *Amos and Andy*. He read to me a lot, stories and poetry, and taught me to memorize many of the poems. He was quite proud that I could recite *The Night before Christmas* by the time I was three. He also taught me a few slightly off color limericks and would laugh and laugh when I gave my little performances. He took me to the circus every time it set up the big top in our town. My Daddy was fun! Whether he was carving the Thanksgiving turkey or Christmas ham, "killing" the Fourth of July watermelon, making snow ice cream, putting soot on his lips and giving me a big Santa kiss while I slept on Christmas Eve, he seemed to innately know the value of creating family rituals. To me, as with most little girls, my Father was larger than life and he was no push over. The "wait until your father comes home" method of discipline was prevalent and practiced by my parents. I particularly remember one time when I got a spanking from my Daddy every evening for a solid week. We lived in a house next door to a lot where a new telephone company facility was being built. Every day I would sneak over to the site to visit with the construction crew and every night I got a "whippin", which really never hurt physically; and I'm not sure who suffered more emotionally. As I was bent over his knee he would tell me it hurt him more than it did me. In any event, it didn't work; remember that with your children!

After moving to Oklahoma and having three more children, Charles Allen McCall continued to be a faithful father. He never missed my brother's Little League games, any school function, graduation or recital. Daddy taught my brothers to play ball, took them fishing and patiently listened to my grating practice on the upright piano he had bought for me. We "antiqued"(refinished) that piano together, his idea. He taught us to ride bikes and to drive a car. Alice Anne was only nine when Grandpa Charlie died and missed out on the driving lessons, but there is a special memory of her and my Father in a car. When she was a toddler, a ritual the two of them had was to go get an "ICEE" at the convenience store near our house. He loved to load her into the front seat where she would stand beside him as he started the car and drove, moving her little body to and fro saying "zzzuudin, zzzuudin," imitating the sound of the engine. I don't know who had more fun, my baby sister or our Dad. Grandpa Charlie instilled in us the values of hard work and education, constantly monitoring our grades and expecting excellence. Daddy didn't like us missing school. One day, not long after we moved to Oklahoma, Mama had allowed me to stay home since I was feeling sick. When Daddy came home for lunch he was unconvinced of the validity of my condition. He came to my room, pulled a chair up to the edge of my bed and proceeded to spoon feed me Chicken Noodle soup. Well after a few spoonfuls of that soup, I threw up all over him. I got to stay home, but I had gotten the message! He was not asking anything of us that he did not demand of himself. I never remember my Father missing a day of work or complaining about having to earn a living. He provided well for us and we really never lacked for anything. Grandpa Charlie's lifelong career was with the United States Army

Artillery Board, Ft. Sill, Oklahoma, serving in a Civil Service position as an ordinance engineer. He helped develop and test weapons for military. He was highly respected in his field and received numerous commendations and promotions, becoming one of the highest ranking Civil Service employees in the nation before his retirement. Daddy took us on frequent outings to the Wichita Mountains Wildlife Refuge to see the buffalo and prairie dog town. Sometimes, since he had keys to the firing ranges through his work, he would unlock the gates and, much to my Mother's horror, drive us over the bumpy, dusty military testing sites of Ft. Sill. Since he worked for the military, Daddy kept a regular schedule, always home for lunch and family suppers in the evening. He did all the grocery shopping, and while Mother did most of the cooking, he had his specialties — a batch of banana or apple fritters, Grandma Delphie's potato salad, fried oysters and, of course, the classic grill foods, steaks, hamburgers and hot dogs. Grandpa Charlie traveled quite often in his work, and he usually came back with a special souvenir for each one of us. The last one I remember getting was a black and white polka dot bikini from Germany! Some of my most vivid memories of my Father are of him standing on the ground above the storm cellar, where he had safely deposited us, watching those Oklahoma tornados coming toward him. I couldn't decide if he was fearless or crazy! One of our family rituals was the three day drive in the midst of summer back to the North Carolina mountains. I can still see Daddy behind the wheel of his big Chrysler sedan, driving and smoking. Like his father, Grandpa Charlie was a heavy smoker throughout his life. When not engaged in activities with his children, he loved to keep his lawn and flower garden, taking particular pride in his spectacular, brightly colored dahlias. He remained an avid reader throughout his life and never lost his interest in the affairs of state. My Father was a humble man, a quiet man of few words, but when he spoke, we listened. Allen had a classic experience during his teenage years which illustrates this trait. One night he had been out with his friends and lost his keys, among other things. He tried to sneak into the house from the back through a den sliding glass door. Mother heard the noise and sent Daddy to check things out. When Allen heard Dad's footsteps coming down the hall, he hid behind the sofa, or at least he though he did. When Daddy flipped on the lights, Allen was crunched in the middle of the room in a somewhat compromised state. (You can ask Judge McCall to elaborate!). Well the words out of my Father's mouth went something like this, "Son, next time ring the doorbell or you may get shot." Then he turned around and went back to bed having never raised his voice. There are many more stories of your Grandfather that your parents or aunts and uncles can share with you. I hope these recollections of mine were meaningful and helped paint the portrait of Grandpa Charlie in your mind's eye.

As I write these words, it is Memorial Day, 2010, and I am thinking a lot about my Father and all who have served and given their lives for our country. Through the years, we have honored our heroes, buried our dead and cared for our wounded. Your Grandfather left home for war and returned a hero, physically unharmed, but still wounded. I vividly remember when I was a teenager getting ready to go to Methodist Youth Fellowship and Church on a Sunday night, my Daddy asking me "How can you believe in a God that allows the horrible things that I saw in the war to happen?" That was really the only time he ever mentioned his war experience to me, but I remember it as if it were yesterday. I also remember my total feeling of emptiness and sadness at not being able to respond to his heartfelt and profound spiritual question. My Father was deeply troubled, today we would say he had Post Traumatic Stress Disorder. But there was no psychological diagnosis of PTSD until the Vietnam War, leaving my Father and all of us, his loved ones, with no name for his and our suffering. I believe there are many others like him who returned from World War II never the same, broken in spirit. They kept silent, lead functional lives, worked hard, raised families, all the while aching inside, as if a piece of their soul had been ripped from their being, leaving a cavernous wound that never healed. I only began to understand the horrors of WWII when I saw *Saving Private Ryan* soon after the movie was released. The theatre was packed and I ended up sitting in the second seat from the right wall. In the seat between me and the wall sat a gentleman who I guessed to be about Grandpa Charlie's age. He had chosen a very private seat, he could have had any one in the row before we arrived. My Father had been dead a long time then, but somehow I had the feeling that this man, this stranger was connected to him and to me. Throughout the movie, he cried and I cried. We never spoke, but I felt that this was his catharsis and I was there to bear witness and that Grandpa Charlie's spirit was beside me. In many ways Charles Allen McCall's story is the story of every American young man who ever went off to war. Today, especially, I remember and honor him and all who serve and have served in the United States Military.

To paraphrase Shakespeare, 'The suffering that men do lives after them; The good is oft interred with their bones.' Most of you know about Grandpa Charlie's brokenness, his lifelong struggle with alcoholism, ultimately losing the battle on October 20, 1975 at age fifty-six, to this disease and lung cancer. I believe that he, along with thousands of other WWII veterans, coped with PTSD by self medicating with alcohol. What else were they to do to deal with the agitation, nervousness, nightmares, flashbacks and many other manifestations of their trauma? I am eternally grateful to Grandma Delphie for these letters, for they show my Father whole and healthy in body and mind and spirit. That is how I choose to remember him and how I hope you will think of him. One day in the future as you walk to your Grandpa Charlie's grave in the Oak Grove Baptist Cemetery in Quebec, North Carolina, as I pray you will, I want you to remember the essential goodness of Charles Allen McCall found in these letters. Then take a few steps up the gentle hill to the grave of our Grandmother, Delphia Omega Owen McCall, and say thank you for the gift of story she kept all those years for us in *Delphie's Trunk*.